IPython Notebook Essentials

Compute scientific data and execute code interactively
with NumPy and SciPy

L. Felipe Martins

[PACKT] open source ❋
PUBLISHING community experience distilled

BIRMINGHAM - MUMBAI

IPython Notebook Essentials

First published: November 2014

Production reference: 1141114

Published by Packt Publishing Ltd.
Livery Place
35 Livery Street
Birmingham B3 2PB, UK.

ISBN 978-1-78398-834-1

www.packtpub.com

Cover image by Duraid Fatouhi (duraidfatouhi@yahoo.com)

Credits

Author
L. Felipe Martins

Reviewers
Sagar Ahire
Steven D. Essinger, Ph.D.
David Selassie Opoku

Commissioning Editor
Pramila Balan

Acquisition Editor
Nikhil Karkal

Content Development Editor
Sumeet Sawant

Technical Editor
Menza Mathew

Copy Editors
Roshni Banerjee
Sarang Chari

Project Coordinator
Danuta Jones

Proofreaders
Ting Baker
Ameesha Green

Indexers
Monica Ajmera Mehta
Priya Sane

Production Coordinator
Komal Ramchandani

Cover Work
Komal Ramchandani

About the Author

L. Felipe Martins holds a PhD in Applied Mathematics from Brown University and has worked as a researcher and educator for more than 20 years. His research is mainly in the field of applied probability. He has been involved in developing code for the open source homework system WeBWorK, where he wrote a library for the visualization of systems of differential equations. He was supported by an NSF grant for this project. Currently, he is an associate professor in the Department of Mathematics at Cleveland State University, Cleveland, Ohio, where he has developed several courses in Applied Mathematics and Scientific Computing. His current duties include coordinating all first-year Calculus sessions.

He is the author of the blog, *All Things Computing* (http://fxmartins.com).

About the Reviewers

Sagar Ahire is a Master's student in Computer Science. He primarily studies Natural Language Processing using statistical techniques and relies heavily on Python—specifically, the IPython ecosystem for scientific computing. You can find his work at github.com/DJSagarAhire.

> I'd like to thank the community of Python for coming together to develop such an amazing ecosystem around the language itself. Apart from that, I'd like to thank my parents and teachers for supporting me and teaching me new things. Finally, I'd like to thank Packt Publishing for approaching me to work on this book; it has been a wonderful learning experience.

Steven D. Essinger, Ph.D. is a data scientist of Recommender Systems and is working in the playlist team at Pandora in Oakland, California. He holds a PhD in Electrical Engineering and focuses on the development of novel, end-to-end computational pipelines employing machine-learning techniques. Steve has previously worked in the field of biological sciences, developing Bioinformatics pipelines for ecologists. He has also worked as a RF systems engineer and holds numerous patents in wireless product design and RFID.

Steve may be reached via LinkedIn at https://www.linkedin.com/in/sessinger.

David Selassie Opoku is a developer and an aspiring data scientist. He is currently a technology teaching fellow at the Meltwater Entrepreneurial School of Technology, Ghana, where he teaches and mentors young entrepreneurs in software development skills and best practices.

David is a graduate of Swarthmore College, Pennsylvania, with a BA in Biology, and he is also a graduate of the New Jersey Institute of Technology with an MS in Computer Science.

David has had the opportunity to work with the Boyce Thompson Institute for Plant Research, the Eugene Lang Center for Civic and Social Responsibility, UNICEF Health Section, and a tech start-up in New York City. He loves Jesus, spending time with family and friends, and tinkering with data and systems.

David may be reached via LinkedIn at `https://www.linkedin.com/in/sdopoku`.

www.PacktPub.com

Support files, eBooks, discount offers, and more

For support files and downloads related to your book, please visit www.PacktPub.com.

Did you know that Packt offers eBook versions of every book published, with PDF and ePub files available? You can upgrade to the eBook version at www.PacktPub.com and as a print book customer, you are entitled to a discount on the eBook copy. Get in touch with us at service@packtpub.com for more details.

At www.PacktPub.com, you can also read a collection of free technical articles, sign up for a range of free newsletters and receive exclusive discounts and offers on Packt books and eBooks.

http://PacktLib.PacktPub.com

Do you need instant solutions to your IT questions? PacktLib is Packt's online digital book library. Here, you can search, access, and read Packt's entire library of books.

Why subscribe?

- Fully searchable across every book published by Packt
- Copy and paste, print, and bookmark content
- On demand and accessible via a web browser

Free access for Packt account holders

If you have an account with Packt at www.PacktPub.com, you can use this to access PacktLib today and view 9 entirely free books. Simply use your login credentials for immediate access.

"To my wife, Ieda Rodrigues, and my wonderful daughters, Laura and Diana."

Table of Contents

Preface   **1**

Chapter 1: A Tour of the IPython Notebook   **7**

Getting started with Anaconda or Wakari   **8**

Installing Anaconda   8

Running the notebook   **8**

Creating a Wakari account   10

Creating your first notebook   11

Example – the coffee cooling problem   **12**

Exercises   **22**

Summary   **22**

Chapter 2: The Notebook Interface   **23**

Editing and navigating a notebook   **23**

Getting help and interrupting computations   25

The Edit mode   25

The Command mode   28

Cell types   29

IPython magics   **33**

Interacting with the operating system   **37**

Saving the notebook   37

Converting the notebook to other formats   38

Running shell commands   39

Running scripts, loading data, and saving data   **41**

Running Python scripts   41

Running scripts in other languages   43

Loading and saving data   45

The rich display system	**47**
Images and YouTube videos	47
HTML	49
Summary	**52**
Chapter 3: Graphics with matplotlib	**53**
The plot function	**54**
Adding a title, labels, and a legend	59
Text and annotations	62
Three-dimensional plots	**66**
Animations	**71**
Summary	**77**
Chapter 4: Handling Data with pandas	**79**
The Series class	**79**
The DataFrame class	**88**
Computational and graphics tools	**95**
An example with a realistic dataset	**101**
Summary	**108**
Chapter 5: Advanced Computing with SciPy, Numba, and NumbaPro	**109**
Overview of SciPy	**109**
Advanced mathematical algorithms with SciPy	**111**
Solving equations and finding optimal values	111
Calculus and differential equations	117
Accelerating computations with Numba and NumbaPro	**128**
Summary	**138**
Appendix A: IPython Notebook Reference Card	**139**
Starting the notebook	**139**
Keyboard shortcuts	**139**
Shortcuts in the Edit mode	139
Shortcuts in the Command mode	140
Importing modules	**141**
Getting help	**141**
Appendix B: A Brief Review of Python	**143**
Introduction	**143**
Basic types, expressions, and variables and their assignment	**143**
Sequence types	**147**
Lists	147
Tuples	150
Strings	151

Dictionaries | **152**
Control structures | **152**
Functions, objects, and methods | 156
Functions | 156
Objects and methods | 158
Summary | **159**
Appendix C: NumPy Arrays | **161**
Introduction | **161**
Array creation and member access | **161**
Indexing and Slicing | **164**
Index | **167**

Preface

The world of computing has seen an incredible revolution in the past 30 years. Not so long ago, high-performance computations required expensive hardware; proprietary software costing hundreds, if not thousands, of dollars; knowledge of computer languages such as FORTRAN, C, or C++; and familiarity with specialized libraries. Even after obtaining the proper hardware and software, just setting up a working environment for advanced scientific computing and data handling was a serious challenge. Many engineers and scientists were forced to become operating systems wizards just to be able to maintain the toolset required by their daily computational work.

Scientists, engineers, and programmers were quick to address this issue. Hardware costs decreased as performance went up, and there was a great push to develop scripting languages that allowed integration of disparate libraries through multiple platforms. It was in this environment that Python was being developed in the late 1980s, under the leadership of Guido Van Rossum. From the beginning, Python was designed to be a cutting-edge, high-level computer language with a simple enough structure that its basics could be quickly learned even by programmers who are not experts.

One of Python's attractive features for rapid development was its interactive shell, through which programmers could experiment with concepts interactively before including them in scripts. However, the original Python shell had a limited set of features and better interactivity was necessary. Starting from 2001, Fernando Perez started developing IPython, an improved interactive Python shell designed specifically for scientific computing.

Since then, IPython has grown to be a full-fledged computational environment built on top of Python. One of most exciting developments is the IPython notebook, a web-based interface for computing with Python. In this book, the reader is guided to a thorough understanding of the notebook's capabilities in easy steps. In the course of learning about the notebook interface, the reader will learn the essential features of several tools, such as NumPy for efficient array-based computations, matplotlib for professional-grade graphics, pandas for data handling and analysis, and SciPy for scientific computation. The presentation is made fun and lively by the introduction of applied examples related to each of the topics. Last but not least, we introduce advanced methods for using GPU-based parallelized computations.

We live in exciting computational times. The combination of inexpensive but powerful hardware and advanced libraries easily available through the IPython notebook provides unprecedented power. We expect that our readers will be as motivated as we are to explore this brave new computational world.

What this book covers

Chapter 1, *A Tour of the IPython Notebook*, shows how to quickly get access to the IPython notebook by either installing the Anaconda distribution or connecting online through Wakari. You will be given an introductory example highlighting some of the exciting features of the notebook interface.

Chapter 2, *The Notebook Interface*, is an in-depth look into the notebook, covering navigation, interacting with the operating system, running scripts, and loading and saving data. Last but not least, we discuss IPython's Rich Display System, which allows the inclusion of a variety of media in the notebook.

Chapter 3, *Graphics with matplotlib*, shows how to create presentation-quality graphs with the matplotlib library. After reading this chapter, you will be able to make two- and three-dimensional plots of data and build animations in the notebook.

Chapter 4, *Handling Data with pandas*, shows how to use the pandas library for data handling and analysis. The main data structures provided by the library are studied in detail, and the chapter shows how to access, insert, and modify data. Data analysis and graphical displays of data are also introduced in this chapter.

Chapter 5, *Advanced Computing with SciPy, Numba, and NumbaPro*, presents advanced computational tools and algorithms that are accessible through SciPy. Acceleration techniques using the libraries Numba and NumbaPro, including use of the GPU for parallelization, are also covered.

Appendix A, IPython Notebook Reference Card, discusses about how to start the Notebook, the keyboard Shortcuts in the Edit and Command modes, how to import modules, and how to access the various Help options.

Appendix B, A Brief Review of Python, gives readers an overview of the Python syntax and features, covering basic types, expressions, variables and assignment, basic data structures, functions, objects and methods.

Appendix C, NumPy Arrays, gives us an introduction about NumPy arrays, and shows us how to create arrays and accessing the members of the array, finally about Indexing and Slicing.

What you need for this book

To run the examples in this book, the following are required:

- Operating system:
    - ° Windows 7 or above, 32- or 64-bit versions.
    - ° Mac OS X 10.5 or above, 64-bit version.
    - ° Linux-based operating systems, such as Ubuntu desktop 14.04 and above, 32- or 64-bit versions.

 Note that 64-bit versions are recommended if available.

- Software:
    - ° Anaconda Python Distribution, version 3.4 or above (available at `http://continuum.io/downloads`)

Who this book is for

This book is for software developers, engineers, scientists, and students who need a quick introduction to the IPython notebook for use in scientific computing, data handling, and analysis, creation of graphical displays, and efficient computations.

It is assumed that the reader has some familiarity with programming in Python, but the essentials of the Python syntax are covered in the appendices and all programming concepts are explained in the text.

If you are looking for a well-paced introduction to the IPython notebook with a lot of applications and code samples, this book is for you.

Conventions

In this book, you will find a number of styles of text that distinguish between different kinds of information. Here are some examples of these styles, and an explanation of their meaning.

Code words in text, database table names, folder names, filenames, file extensions, pathnames, dummy URLs, user input, and Twitter handles are shown as follows: "The simplest way to run IPython is to issue the `ipython` command in a terminal window."

A block of code is set as follows:

```
temp_coffee = 185.
temp_cream = 40.
vol_coffee = 8.
vol_cream = 1.
initial_temp_mix_at_shop = temp_mixture(temp_coffee, vol_coffee, temp_cream, vol_cream)
temperatures_mix_at_shop = cooling_law(initial_temp_mix_at_shop, times)
temperatures_mix_at_shop
```

When we wish to draw your attention to a particular part of a code block, the relevant lines or items are set in bold:

```
[default]
temp_coffee = 185.
temp_cream = 40.
vol_coffee = 8.
vol_cream = 1.
initial_temp_mix_at_shop = temp_mixture(temp_coffee, vol_coffee, temp_cream, vol_cream)
temperatures_mix_at_shop = cooling_law(initial_temp_mix_at_shop, times)
temperatures_mix_at_shop
```

Any command-line input or output is written as follows:

```
ipython notebook
```

New terms and important words are shown in bold. Words that you see on the screen, in menus or dialog boxes for example, appear in the text like this: "Simply, click on the **New Notebook** button to create a new notebook."

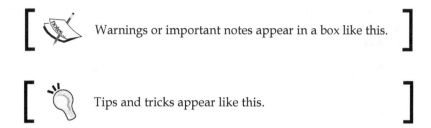

Warnings or important notes appear in a box like this.

Tips and tricks appear like this.

Reader feedback

Feedback from our readers is always welcome. Let us know what you think about this book—what you liked or may have disliked. Reader feedback is important for us to develop titles that you really get the most out of.

To send us general feedback, simply send an e-mail to feedback@packtpub.com, and mention the book title via the subject of your message.

If there is a topic that you have expertise in and you are interested in either writing or contributing to a book, see our author guide on www.packtpub.com/authors.

Customer support

Now that you are the proud owner of a Packt book, we have a number of things to help you to get the most from your purchase.

Errata

Although we have taken every care to ensure the accuracy of our content, mistakes do happen. If you find a mistake in one of our books—maybe a mistake in the text or the code—we would be grateful if you would report this to us. By doing so, you can save other readers from frustration and help us improve subsequent versions of this book. If you find any errata, please report them by visiting http://www.packtpub.com/submit-errata, selecting your book, clicking on the **errata submission form** link, and entering the details of your errata. Once your errata are verified, your submission will be accepted and the errata will be uploaded on our website, or added to any list of existing errata, under the Errata section of that title. Any existing errata can be viewed by selecting your title from http://www.packtpub.com/support.

Piracy

Piracy of copyright material on the Internet is an ongoing problem across all media. At Packt, we take the protection of our copyright and licenses very seriously. If you come across any illegal copies of our works, in any form, on the Internet, please provide us with the location address or website name immediately so that we can pursue a remedy.

Please contact us at copyright@packtpub.com with a link to the suspected pirated material.

We appreciate your help in protecting our authors, and our ability to bring you valuable content.

Questions

You can contact us at questions@packtpub.com if you are having a problem with any aspect of the book, and we will do our best to address it.

1
A Tour of the IPython Notebook

This chapter gives a brief introduction to the **IPython notebook** and highlights some of its special features that make it a great tool for scientific and data-oriented computing. IPython notebooks use a standard text format that makes it easy to share results.

After the quick installation instructions, you will learn how to start the notebook and be able to immediately use IPython to perform computations. This simple, initial setup is all that is needed to take advantage of the many notebook features, such as interactively producing high quality graphs, performing advanced technical computations, and handling data with specialized libraries.

All examples are explained in detail in this book and available online. We do not expect the readers to have deep knowledge of Python, but readers unfamiliar with the Python syntax can consult *Appendix B, A Brief Review of Python*, for an introduction/refresher.

In this chapter, we will cover the following topics:

- Getting started with Anaconda or Wakari
- Creating notebooks and then learning about the basics of editing and executing statements
- An applied example highlighting the notebook features

Getting started with Anaconda or Wakari

There are several approaches to setting up an IPython notebook environment. We suggest you use Anaconda, a free distribution designed for large-scale data processing, predictive analytics, and scientific computing. Alternatively, you can use Wakari, which is a web-based installation of Anaconda. Wakari has several levels of service, but the basic level is free and suitable for experimenting and learning.

 We recommend that you set up both a Wakari account and a local Anaconda installation. Wakari has the functionality of easy sharing and publication. This local installation does not require an Internet connection and may be more responsive. Thus, you get the best of both worlds!

Installing Anaconda

To install Anaconda on your computer, perform the following steps:

1. Download Anaconda for your platform from `https://store.continuum.io/cshop/anaconda/`.

2. After the file is completely downloaded, install Anaconda:

   ○ Windows users can double-click on the installer and follow the on-screen instruction

   ○ Mac users can double-click the `.pkg` file and follow the instructions displayed on screen

   ○ Linux users can run the following command:

   ```
   bash <downloaded file>
   ```

 Anaconda supports several different versions of Python. This book assumes you are using Version 2.7, which is the standard version that comes with Anaconda. The most recent version of Python, Version 3.0, is significantly different and is just starting to gain popularity. Many Python packages are still only fully supported in Version 2.7.

Running the notebook

You are now ready to run the notebook. First, we create a directory named `my_notebooks` to hold your notebooks and open a terminal window at this directory. Different operating systems perform different steps.

Microsoft Windows users need to perform the following steps:

1. Open Window Explorer.
2. Navigate to the location where your notebooks are stored.
3. Click on the **New Folder** button.
4. Rename the folder `my_notebooks`.
5. Right-click on the `my_notebooks` folder and select **Open command window here** from the context menu.

Mac OS X and other Unix-like systems' users need to perform the following steps:

1. Open a terminal window.
2. Run the following commands:

    ```
    mkdir my_notebooks
    cd my_notebooks
    ```

3. Then, execute the following command on the terminal window:

    ```
    ipython notebook
    ```

After a while, your browser will automatically load the notebook dashboard as shown in the following screenshot. The dashboard is a mini filesystem where you can manage your notebooks. The notebooks listed in the dashboard correspond exactly to the files you have in the directory where the notebook server was launched.

Internet Explorer does not fully support all features in the IPython notebook. It is suggested that you use Chrome, Firefox, Safari, Opera, or another standards-conforming browser. If your default browser is one of those, you are ready to go. Alternatively, close the Internet Explorer notebook, open a compatible browser, and enter the notebook address given in the command window from which you started IPython. This will be something like `http://127.0.0.1:8888` for the first notebook you open.

Creating a Wakari account

To access Wakari, simply go to `https://www.wakari.io` and create an account. After logging in, you will be automatically directed to an introduction to using the notebook interface in Wakari. This interface is shown in the following screenshot:

The interface elements as seen in the preceding screenshot are described as follows:

- The section marked **1** shows the directory listing of your notebooks and files. On the top of this area, there is a toolbar with buttons to create new files and directories as well as download and upload files.

- The section marked **2** shows the **Welcome to Wakari** notebook. This is the initial notebook with information about IPython and Wakari. The notebook interface is discussed in detail in *Chapter 2, The Notebook Interface*.

- The section marked **3** shows the Wakari toolbar. This has the **New Notebook** button and drop-down menus with other tools.

This book concentrates on using IPython through the notebook interface. However, it's worth mentioning the two other ways to run IPython.

The simplest way to run IPython is to issue the `ipython` command in a terminal window. This starts a command-line session of IPython. As the reader may have guessed, this is the original interface for IPython.

Alternatively, IPython can be started using the `ipython qtconsole` command. This starts an IPython session attached to a QT window. QT is a popular multiplatform windowing system that is bundled with the Anaconda distribution. These alternatives may be useful in systems that, for some reason, do not support the notebook interface.

Creating your first notebook

We are ready to create our first notebook! Simply click on the **New Notebook** button to create a new notebook.

- In a local notebook installation, the **New Notebook** button appears in the upper-left corner of the dashboard.

- In Wakari, the **New Notebook** button is at the top of the dashboard, in a distinct color. *Do not* use the **Add File** button.

Notice that the Wakari dashboard contains a directory list on the left. You can use this to organize your notebooks in any convenient way you choose. Wakari actually provides access to a fully working Linux shell.

We are now ready to start computing. The notebook interface is displayed in the following screenshot:

By default, new notebooks are named `UntitledX`, where `X` is a number. To change it, just click on the current title and edit the dialog that pops up.

At the top of the notebook, you will see an empty box with the `In [ ]:` text on the left-hand side. This box is called a **code cell** and it is where the IPython shell commands are entered. Usually, the first command we issue in a new notebook is `%pylab inline`. Go ahead and type this line in the code cell and then press *Shift + Enter* (this is the most usual way to execute commands. Simply pressing *Enter* will create a new line in the current cell.) Once executed, this command will issue a message as follows:

`Populating the interactive namespace from numpy and matplotlib`

This command makes several computational tools easily available and is the recommended way to use the IPython notebook for interactive computations. The `inline` directive tells IPython that we want graphics embedded in the notebook and not rendered with an external program.

Commands that start with `%` and `%%` are called **magic** commands and are used to set up configuration options and special features. The `%pylab` magic command imports a large collection of names into the IPython namespace. This command is usually frowned upon for causing **namespace pollution**. The recommended way to use libraries in scripts is to use the following command:

`import numpy as np`

Then, for example, to access the `arange()` function in the `NumPy` package, one uses `np.arange()`. The problem with this approach is that it becomes cumbersome to use common mathematical functions, such as `sin()`, `cos()`, and so on. These would have to be entered as `np.sin()`, `np.cos()`, and so on, which makes the notebook much less readable.

In this book, we adopt the following middle-of-the road convention: when doing interactive computations, we will use the `%pylab` directive to make it easier to type formulae. However, when using other libraries or writing scripts, we will use the recommended best practices to import libraries.

Example – the coffee cooling problem

Suppose you get a cup of coffee at a coffee shop. Should you mix the cream into the coffee at the shop or wait until you reach your office? The goal, we assume, is to have the coffee as hot as possible. So, the main question is how the coffee is going to cool as you walk back to the office.

The difference between the two strategies of mixing cream is:

- If you pour the cream at the shop, there is a sudden drop of temperature *before* the coffee starts to cool down as you walk back to the office

- If you pour the cream after getting back to the office, the sudden drop occurs *after* the cooling period during the walk

We need a model for the cooling process. The simplest such model is Newton's cooling law, which states that the rate of cooling is proportional to the temperature difference between the coffee in the cup and the ambient temperature. This reflects the intuitive notion that, for example, if the outside temperature is 40°F, the coffee cools faster than if it is 50°F. This assumption leads to a well-known formula for the way the temperature changes:

$$T_{\text{final}} = T_{\text{outside}} + (T_{\text{start}} - T_{\text{outside}})r^{\text{walk time}}$$

The constant *r* is a number between 0 and 1, representing the heat exchange between the coffee cup and the outside environment. This constant depends on several factors, and may be hard to estimate without experimentation. We just chose it somewhat arbitrarily in this first example.

We will start by setting variables to represent the outside temperature and the rate of cooling and defining a function that computes the temperatures as the liquid cools. Then, type the lines of code representing the cooling law in a single code cell. Press *Enter* or click on **Return** to add new lines to the cell.

As discussed, we will first define the variables to hold the outside temperature and the rate of cooling:

```
temp_out = 70.0
r = 0.9
```

After entering the preceding code on the cell, press *Shift + Enter* to execute the cell. Notice that after the cell is executed, a new cell is created.

Notice that we entered the value of temp_out as 70.0 even though the value is an integer in this case. This is not strictly necessary in this case, but it is considered good practice. Some code may behave differently, depending on whether it operates on integer or floating-point variables. For example, evaluating 20/8 in Python Version 2.7 results in 2, which is the integer quotient of 20 divided by 8. On the other hand, 20.0/8.0 evaluates to the floating-point value 2.5. By forcing the variable temp_out to be a floating-point value, we prevent this somewhat unexpected kind of behavior.

A second reason is to simply improve code clarity and readability. A reader of the notebook on seeing the value 70.0 will easily understand that the variable temp_out represents a real number. So, it becomes clear that a value of 70.8, for example, would also be acceptable for the outside temperature.

Next, we define the function representing the cooling law:

```
def cooling_law(temp_start, walk_time):

    return temp_out + (temp_start - temp_out) * r ** walk_time
```

Please be careful with the way the lines are indented, since indentation is used by Python to define code blocks. Again, press *Shift + Enter* to execute the cell.

The cooling_law() function accepts the starting temperature and walking time as the input and returns the final temperature of the coffee. Notice that we are only defining the function, so no output is produced. In our examples, we will always choose meaningful names for variables. To be consistent, we use the conventions in the Google style of coding for Python as shown in http://google-styleguide.googlecode.com/svn/trunk/pyguide.html#Python_Language_Rules.

Notice that the exponentiation (power) operator in Python is ** and not ^ as in other mathematical software. If you get the following error when trying to compute a power, it is likely that you meant to use the ** operator:

```
TypeError: unsupported operand type(s) for ^:
'float' and 'float'
```

We can now compute the effect of cooling given any starting temperature and walking time. For example, to compute the temperature of the coffee after 10 minutes, assuming the initial temperature to be 185°F, run the following code in a cell:

```
cooling_law(185.0, 10.0)
```

The corresponding output is:

```
110.0980206115
```

What if we want to know what the final temperature for several walking times is? For example, suppose that we want to compute the final temperature every 5 minutes up to 20 minutes. This is where NumPy makes things easy:

```
times = arange(0.,21.,5.)
temperatures = cooling_law(185., times)
temperatures
```

We start by defining `times` to be a NumPy array, using the `arange()` function. This function takes three arguments: the starting value of the range, the ending value of the range, and the increment.

You may be wondering why the ending value of the range is 21 and not 20. It's a common convention in Computer Science, followed by Python. *When a range is specified, the right endpoint never belongs to the range.* So, if we had specified 20 as the right endpoint, the range would only contain the values 0, 5, 10, and 15.

After defining the `times` array, we can simply call the `cooling_law()` function with `times` as the second argument. This computes the temperatures at the given times.

You may have noticed that there is something strange going on here. The first time the `cooling_law()` function was called, the second argument was a floating-point number. The second time, it was a NumPy array. This is possible thanks to Python's dynamic typing and polymorphism. NumPy redefines the arithmetic operators to work with arrays in a smart way. So, we do not need to define a new function especially for this case.

Once we have the temperatures, we can display them in a graph. To display the graph, execute the following command line in a cell:

```
plot(times, temperatures, 'o')
```

The preceding command line produces the following plot:

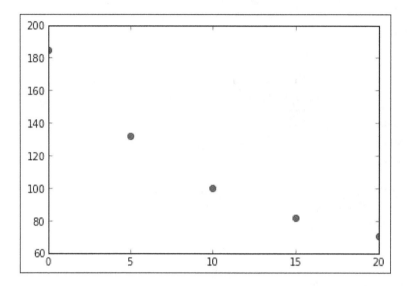

The `plot()` function is a part of the `matplotlib` package, which will be studied in detail in *Chapter 3, Graphics with matplotlib*. In this example, the first two arguments to `plot()` are `NumPy` arrays that specify the data for the horizontal and vertical axes, respectively. The third argument specifies the plot symbol to be a filled circle.

We are now ready to tackle the original problem: should we mix the cream in at the coffee shop or wait until we get back to the office? When we mix the cream, there is a sudden drop in temperature. The temperature of the mixture is the average of the temperature of the two liquids, weighted by volume. The following code defines a function to compute the resulting temperature in a mix:

```
def temp_mixture(t1, v1, t2, v2):
    return (t1 * v1 + t2 * v2) / (v1 + v2)
```

The arguments in the function are the temperature and volume of each liquid. Using this function, we can now compute the temperature evolution when the cream is added at the coffee shop:

```
temp_coffee = 185.
temp_cream = 40.
```

```
vol_coffee = 8.
```

```
vol_cream = 1.
```

```
initial_temp_mix_at_shop = temp_mixture(temp_coffee, vol_coffee, temp_cream, vol_cream)
```

```
temperatures_mix_at_shop = cooling_law(initial_temp_mix_at_shop, times)
```

```
temperatures_mix_at_shop
```

 Notice that we repeat the variable `temperatures_mix_at_shop` at the end of the cell. This is not a typo. The IPython notebook, by default, assumes that the output of a cell is the last expression computed in the cell. It is a common idiom to list the variables one wants to have displayed, at the end of the cell. We will later see how to display fancier, nicely formatted output.

As usual, type all the commands in a single code cell and then press *Shift + Enter* to run the whole cell. We first set the initial temperatures and volumes for the coffee and the cream. Then, we call the `temp_mixture()` function to calculate the initial temperature of the mixture. Finally, we use the `cooling_law()` function to compute the temperatures for different walking times, storing the result in the `temperatures_mix_at_shop` variable. The preceding command lines produce the following output:

```
array([ 168.88888889,  128.3929    ,  104.48042352,   90.36034528,
         82.02258029])
```

Remember that the `times` array specifies times from 0 to 20 with intervals of 5 minutes. So, the preceding output gives the temperatures at these times, assuming that the cream was mixed in the shop.

To compute the temperatures when considering that the cream is mixed after walking back to our office, execute the following commands in the cell:

```
temperatures_unmixed_coffee = cooling_law(temp_coffee, times)
```

```
temperatures_mix_at_office = temp_mixture(temperatures_unmixed_coffee, vol_coffee, temp_cream, vol_cream)
```

```
temperatures_mix_at_office
```

We again use the `cooling_law()` function, but using the initial coffee temperature `temp_coffee` (without mixing the cream) as the first input variable. We store the results in the `temperatures_unmixed_coffee` variable.

To compute the effect of mixing the cream in after walking, we call the `temp_mixture()` function. Notice that the main difference in the two computations is the order in which the functions `cooling_law()` and `temp_mixture()` are called. The preceding command lines produce the following output:

```
array([ 168.88888889,  127.02786667,  102.30935165,   87.71331573,
         79.09450247])
```

Let's now plot the two temperature arrays. Execute the following command lines in a single cell:

```
plot(times, temperatures_mix_at_shop, 'o')
plot(times, temperatures_mix_at_office, 'D', color='r')
```

The first `plot()` function call is the same as before. The second is similar, but we want the plotting symbol to be a filled diamond, indicated by the argument `'D'`. The `color='r'` option makes the markings red. This produces the following plot:

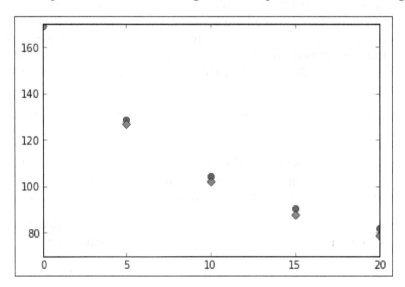

Notice that, by default, all graphs created in a single code cell will be drawn on the same set of axes. As a conclusion, we can see that, for the data parameters used in this example, mixing the cream at the coffee shop is always better no matter what the walking time is. The reader should feel free to change the parameters and observe what happens in different situations.

Scientific plots should make clear what is being represented, the variables being plotted, as well as the units being used. This can be nicely handled by adding annotations to the plot. It is fairly easy to add annotations in `matplotlib`, as shown in the following code:

```
plot(times, temperatures_mix_at_shop, 'o')
plot(times, temperatures_mix_at_office, 'D', color='r')
title('Coffee temperatures for different walking times')
xlabel('Waking time (min)')
ylabel('Temperature (F)')
legend(['Mix at shop', 'Mix at office'])
```

After plotting the arrays again, we call the appropriate functions to add the title (`title()`), horizontal axis label (`xlabel()`), vertical axis label (`ylabel()`), and legend (`legend()`). The arguments to all this functions are strings or a list of strings as in the case of `legend()`. The following graph is what we get as an output for the preceding command lines:

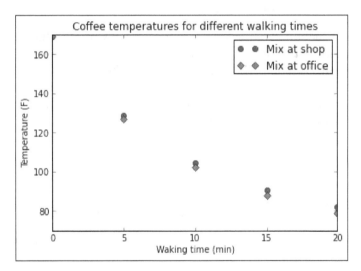

There is something unsatisfactory about the way we conducted this analysis; our office, supposedly, is at a fixed distance from the coffee shop. The main factor in the situation is the outside temperature. Should we use different strategies during summer and winter? In order to investigate this, we start by defining a function that accepts as input both the cream temperature and outside temperature. The return value of the function is the difference of final temperatures when we get back to the office.

The function is defined as follows:

```
temp_coffee = 185.
vol_coffee = 8.
vol_cream = 1.
walk_time = 10.0
r = 0.9
def temperature_difference(temp_cream, temp_out):
    temp_start = temp_mixture(temp_coffee,vol_coffee,temp_cream,vol_
cream)
    temp_mix_at_shop = temp_out + (temp_start - temp_out) * r ** walk_
time
    temp_start = temp_coffee
    temp_unmixed =  temp_out + (temp_start - temp_out) * r ** walk_time
    temp_mix_at_office = temp_mixture(temp_unmixed, vol_coffee, temp_
cream, vol_cream)
    return temp_mix_at_shop - temp_mix_at_office
```

In the preceding function, we first set the values of the variables that will be considered constant in the analysis, that is, the temperature of the coffee, the volumes of coffee and cream, the walking time, and the rate of cooling. Then, we defined the `temperature_difference` function using the same formulas we discussed previously. We can now use this function to compute a matrix with the temperature differences for several different values of the cream temperature and outside temperature:

```
cream_temperatures = arange(40.,51.,1.)
outside_temperatures = arange(35.,60.,1.)
cream_values, outside_values = meshgrid(cream_temperatures, outside_
temperatures)
temperature_differences = temperature_difference(cream_values, outside_
values)
```

The first two lines in the cell use the `arange()` function to define arrays that contain equally spaced values for the cream temperatures and outside temperatures. We then call the convenience function, `meshgrid()`. This function returns two arrays that are convenient to calculate data for three-dimensional graphs and are stored in the variables `cream_values` and `outside_values`. Finally, we call the `temperature _difference()` function, and store the return value in the `temperature_differences` array. This will be a two-dimensional array (that is, a matrix).

We are now ready to create a three dimensional plot of the temperature differences:

```
from mpl_toolkits.mplot3d import Axes3D
fig = figure()
fig.set_size_inches(7,5)
ax = fig.add_subplot(111, projection='3d')
ax.plot_surface(cream_values, outside_values, temperature_differences,
rstride=1, cstride=1, cmap=cm.coolwarm, linewidth=0)
xlabel('Cream temperature')
ylabel('Outside temperature')
title('Temperature difference')
```

In the preceding code segment, we started by importing the `Axes3D` class using the following line:

```
from mpl_toolkits.mplot3d import Axes3D
```

This class, located in the `mpl_toolkits.mplot3d` module, is not automatically loaded. So, it must be explicitly imported.

Then we create an object `fig` of the class `figure`, set its size, and generate an object `ax` that is an object of the class `Axes3D`. Finally, we call the `ax.plot_surface()` method to generate the plot. The last three command lines set the axis labels and the title.

In this explanation, we used some terms that are common in object-oriented programming. A Python **object** is simply a data structure that can be handled in some specialized way. Every object is an **instance** of a **class** that defines the object's data. The class also defines **methods**, which are functions specialized to work with objects belonging to the class.

The output of the preceding command lines will produce the following graph:

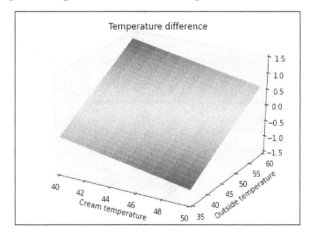

Notice the `cmap=cm.coolwarm` argument in the call to `ax.plot_surface()`. This sets the color map of the plot to `cm.coolwarm`. This color map conveniently uses a blue-red gradient for the function values. As a result, negative temperature differences are shown in blue and positive temperatures in red. Notice that there seems to be a straight line that defines where the temperature difference transitions from negative to positive. This actually corresponds to values where the outside temperature and the cream temperature are equal. It turns out that if the cream temperature is lower than the outside temperature, we should mix the cream into the coffee at the coffee shop. Otherwise, the cream should be poured in the office.

Exercises

The following are some practice questions that will help you to understand and apply the concepts learned in this chapter:

- In our example, we discussed how to determine the cooling rate r. Modify the example to plot the temperature evolution for several values of r, keeping all other variables fixed.

- Search the **matplotlib** documentation at `http://matplotlib.org` to figure out how to generate a contour plot of the temperature differences.

  Our analysis ignores the fact that the cream will also change temperature as we walk. Change the notebook so that this factor is taken into account

Summary

In this chapter, we set up an IPython environment with Anaconda, accessed the IPython notebook online through Wakari, created a notebook, and learned the basics of editing and executing commands, and lastly, we went through an extensively applied example featuring the basic notebook capabilities.

In the next chapter, we will delve more deeply in the facilities provided by the notebook interface—including notebook navigation and editing facilities, interfacing with the operating system, loading and saving data, and running scripts.

2
The Notebook Interface

The IPython notebook has an extensive user interface that makes it appropriate for the creation of richly formatted documents. In this chapter, we will thoroughly explore the notebook's capabilities. We will also consider the pitfalls and best practices of using the notebook.

In this chapter, the following topics will be covered:

- Notebook editing and navigation, which includes cell types; adding, deleting, and moving cells; loading and saving notebooks; and keyboard shortcuts
- IPython magics
- Interacting with the operating system
- Running scripts, loading data, and saving data
- Embedding images, video, and other media with IPython's rich display system

Editing and navigating a notebook

When we open a notebook (by either clicking on its name in the dashboard or creating a new notebook), we see the following in the browser window:

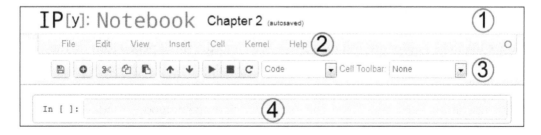

In the preceding screenshot, from the top to the bottom, we see the following components:

- The **Title** bar (area marked **1**) that contains the name of the notebook (in the preceding example, we can see **Chapter 2**) and information about the notebook version

- The **Menu** bar (area marked **2**) looks like a regular application menu

- The **Toolbar** (area marked **3**) is used for quick access to the most frequently used functionality

- In the area marked **4**, an empty computation cell is shown

Starting with IPython Version 2.0, the notebook has two modes of operation:

- **Edit**: In this mode, a single cell comes into focus and we can enter text, execute code, and perform tasks related to that single cell. The Edit mode is activated by clicking on a cell or pressing the *Enter* key.

- **Command**: In this mode, we perform tasks related to the whole notebook structure, such as moving, copying, cutting, and pasting cells. A series of keyboard shortcuts are available to make these operations more efficient. The Command mode is activated by clicking anywhere on the notebook, outside any cell, or by pressing the *Esc* key.

When we open a notebook, it's in the Command mode. Let's enter into the Edit mode in our new notebook. For this, either click on the empty cell or hit *Enter*. The notebook's appearance will change slightly, as shown in the following screenshot:

Notice the thick border around the selected cell and the small pencil icon on the top-right corner of the notebook menu. These indicate that the notebook is in the Edit mode.

In the upcoming subsections, we will explore each of the notebook modes in detail.

Getting help and interrupting computations

The notebook is a complex tool that integrates several different technologies. It is unlikely that new (or even experienced) users will be able to memorize all the commands and shortcuts. The **Help** menu in the notebook has links to relevant documentation that should be consulted as often as necessary.

> Newcomers may want to visit the Notebook Interface Tour, which is available at `http://nbviewer.ipython.org/github/ipython/ipython/blob/2.x/examples/Notebook/User%20Interface.ipynb`, to get started.

It is also easy to get help on any object (including functions and methods). For example, to access help on the `sum()` function, run the following line of code in a cell:

```
sum?
```

Appending `??` to an object's name will provide more detailed information. Incidentally, just running `?` by itself in a cell displays information about IPython features.

The other important thing to know right from the start is how to interrupt a computation. This can be done through the **Kernel** menu, where the kernel process running the notebook code can be interrupted and restarted. The kernel can also be interrupted by clicking on the **Stop** button on the toolbar.

The Edit mode

The Edit mode is used to enter text in cells and to execute code. Let's type some code in the fresh notebook we created. As usual, we want to import NumPy and matplotlib to the current namespace, so we enter the following magic command in the first cell:

```
%pylab inline
```

Press *Shift + Enter* or click on the Play button on the toolbar to execute the code. Notice that either of the options causes a new cell to be added under the current cell.

Just to have something concrete to work with, let's suppose we want to compute the interest accumulated in an investment. Type the following code in three successive cells:

- In cell 1, enter the following command lines:

```
def return_on_investment(principal, interest_rate, number_of_
years):
    return principal * e ** (interest_rate * number_of_years)
```

- In cell 2, enter the following command lines:

```
principal = 250
interest_rate = .034
tstart = 0.0
tend = 5.0
npoints = 6
```

- In cell 3, enter the following command lines:

```
tvalues = linspace(tstart, tend, npoints)
amount_values = return_on_investment(principal, interest_rate,
tvalues)
plot(tvalues, amount_values, 'o')
title('Return on investment, years {} to {}'.format(tstart, tend))
xlabel('Years')
ylabel('Return')
tstart += tend
tend += tend
```

Now, perform the following steps:

1. Run cell 1 and cell 2 in the usual way by pressing *Shift + Enter*.
2. Run cell 3 by pressing *Ctrl + Enter* instead.

Notice that cell 3 continues to be selected after being executed. Keep pressing *Ctrl + Enter* while having cell 3 selected. The plot will be updated each time to display the return on the investment for a different 5-year period.

This is how the code works:

- In cell 1, we defined a function that computes the return on investment for given principal, interest rate, and number of years.

- In cell 2, we set actual values for the principal and interest, and then initialized variables to define the period for which we want to do the computation.

- Cell 3 computed the amount returned for a period of 5 years and plotted the results.

- Then, the variables `tstart` and `tend` were updated. The command lines are as follows:

```
tstart += tend
tend += tend
```

The effect is that, the next time the cell gets updated, time advances to the next 5-year period. So, by repeatedly pressing *Ctrl* + *Enter*, we can quickly see how the investment grows in successive 5-year periods.

There is a third way to run commands in a cell. Select cell 2 again by clicking on it. Then, press *Alt* + *Enter* in Windows or *Option* + *Enter* on a Mac. This will run cell 2 and insert a new cell under it. Leave the new cell alone for a while. We don't really need that cell, and we will learn how to delete it in the next subsection.

So, there are three ways to run the contents of a cell:

- Pressing *Shift* + *Enter* or the Play button on the toolbar. This will run the cell and select the next cell (create a new cell if at the end of the notebook). This is the most usual way to execute a cell.

- Pressing *Ctrl* + *Enter*. This will run the cell and keep the same cell selected. It's useful when we want to repeatedly execute the same cell. For example, if we want to make modifications to the existing code.

- Pressing *Alt* + *Enter*. This will run the cell and insert a new cell immediately below it.

Another useful feature of the Edit mode is **tab completion**. Select an empty cell and type the following command:

```
print am
```

Then, press the *Tab* key. A list of suggested completions appears. Using the arrow keys of the keyboard or the mouse, we can select `amount_values` and then press *Enter* to accept the completion.

A very important feature of IPython is easy access to help information. Click on an empty cell and type:

```
linspace
```

Then, press *Shift + Tab*. A tooltip containing information about the `linspace` function will appear. More information can be obtained by clicking on the **+** symbol at the top-right of the tooltip window. By clicking on the **^** symbol, the information is displayed in an information area at the bottom of the notebook.

The *Tab* and *Shift + Tab* features are the most useful ones of the notebook; be sure to use them often!

The Command mode

The number of shortcuts available in the Command mode is substantially larger than those available in the Edit mode. Fortunately, it is not necessary to memorize all of them at once, since most actions in the Command mode are also available in the menu. In this section, we will only describe some common features of the Command mode. The following table lists some of the useful shortcuts for editing cells; the other shortcuts will be described later:

Shortcut	Action
Enter	Activates the Edit mode
Esc	Activates the Command mode
H	Displays the list of keyboard shortcuts
S or *Ctrl + S*	Saves the notebook
A	Inserts a cell above
B	Inserts a cell below
D (press twice)	Deletes the cell
Z	Undoes the last delete
Ctrl + K	Moves the cell up
Ctrl + J	Moves the cell down
X	Cuts the content of the cell
C	Copies the content of the cell
V	Pastes the content of the cell below the current cell
Shift + V	Pastes the content of the cell above the current cell

One of the most common (and frustrating) mistakes when using the notebook is to type something in the wrong mode. Remember to use *Esc* to switch to the Command mode and *Enter* to switch to the Edit mode. Also, remember that clicking on a cell automatically places it in the Edit mode, so it will be necessary to press *Esc* to go to the Command mode.

Go ahead and try some of the editing shortcuts in the sample notebook. Here is one example that you can try:

1. Press *Esc* to go to the Command mode.

2. Use the arrow keys to move to the empty cell we created between cell 2 and cell 3 in the previous subsection.

3. Press *D* twice. This will cause the cell to be deleted. To get the cell back, press *Z*.

 Notice that some of the shortcuts do not conform to the usual shortcuts in other software. For example, the shortcuts for cutting, copying, and pasting cells are not preceded by the *Ctrl* key.

Cell types

So far, we have used the notebook cells only to enter code. We can, however, use cells to enter the explanatory text and give structure to the notebook. The notebook uses the **Markdown** language to allow easy insertion of rich text in a cell. Markdown was created by John Gruber for plain text editing of HTML. See the project page at `http://daringfireball.net/projects/markdown/basics` for the basics of the syntax.

Let's see how it works in the notebook. If you created any other cells to experiment with the keyboard shortcuts in the previous section, delete them now so that the notebook only has the `%pylab inline` cell and the three cells where the interest computation is done.

Click on the `%pylab inline` cell and insert a cell right below it. You can either use the menu, or go to the Command mode (using the *Esc* key) and use the shortcut key *B*.

We now want to convert the new cell type to Markdown. There are three ways to do that. Start by clicking on the cell to select it, and then perform one of the following steps:

- Click on the notebook menu item **Cell**, select **Cell Type**, and then click on **Markdown** as shown in the following screenshot

- Select **Markdown** from the drop-down box on the notebook's toolbar

- Go to the Command mode by pressing *Esc* and then press *M*

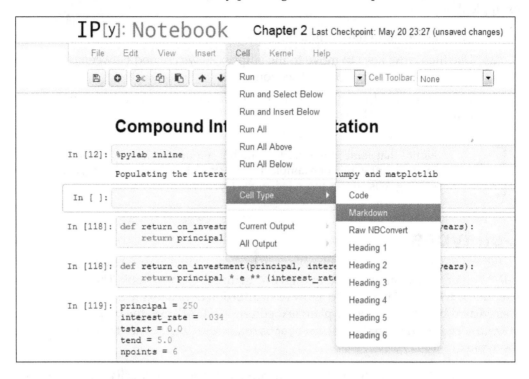

Notice that once the cell is converted to Markdown, it is automatically in the Edit mode. Now, enter the following in the new Markdown cell (be careful to leave an extra blank line where indicated):

```
We want to know how an investment grows with a fixed interest.

The *compound interest* formula states that:
$$R = Pe^{rt}$$
where:

- $P$ is the principal (initial investment).
- $r$ is the annual interest rate, as a decimal.
- $t$ is the time in years.
- $e$ is the base of natural logarithms.
- $R$ is the total return after $t$ years (including principal)

For details, see the [corresponding Wikipedia entry](http://
en.wikipedia.org/wiki/Compound_interest).

We start by defining a Python function that implements this formula.
```

After the text is entered, press *Shift + Enter* to execute the cell. Instead of using the IPython interpreter to evaluate the cell, the notebook runs it through the Markdown interpreter and the cell is rendered using HTML, producing the output displayed in the following screenshot:

We want to know how an investment grows with a fixed interest.

The *compound interest* formula states that:

$$R = Pe^{rt}$$

where:

- P is the principal (initial investment).
- r is the annual interest rate, as a decimal.
- t is the time in years.
- e is the base of natural logarithms.
- R is the total return after t years (including principal)

For details, see the corresponding Wikipedia entry.

We start by defining a Python function that implements this formula.

In this example, we use the following Markdown features:

- Text is entered normally and a new paragraph is indicated by letting an extra blank line within the text.

- Italics are indicated by enclosing the text between asterisks, as in `*compound interest*`.

- Formulae enclosed in double dollar (`$$`) signs, as in `$$R = Pe^{rt}$$`, are displayed centered in the page.

- An unordered list is indicated by lines starting with a dash (`-`). It is important to leave blank lines before and after the list.

- A single dollar (`$`) sign causes the formula to be typeset inline.

- Hyperlinks are specified in the following format: `[corresponding Wikipedia entry]( http://en.wikipedia.org/wiki/Compound_interest)`.

In a Markdown cell, mathematical formulae can be entered in **LaTeX**, which is an extensive language for technical typesetting that is beyond the scope of this book. Fortunately, we don't need to use the full-fledged formatting capabilities of LaTeX, but only the formula-editing features. A good quick introduction to LaTeX can be found at `http://en.wikibooks.org/wiki/LaTeX/Mathematics`. Learning a bit of LaTeX is very useful, since it is also used in other Python libraries. For instance, `matplotlib` allows LaTeX to be used in plot titles and axis labels. In the notebook, LaTeX is rendered by MathJax, a LaTeX interpreter implemented in JavaScript by Davide Cervone. Visit `http://www.mathjax.org/` for details.

To edit the contents of a Markdown cell once it has been displayed, simply double-click on the cell. After the edits are done, run the cell using *Shift + Enter* to render it again.

To add structure to the notebook, we can add headings of different sizes. Let's add a global heading to our notebook:

1. Add a new cell at the very top of the notebook and change its type to **Heading 1**. Recall that there are three alternatives to do this:
   - By navigating to **Cell | Cell Type**
   - Using the **Cell Type** dropdown on the toolbar
   - Using the keyboard shortcut *1* in the Command mode

2. Enter a title for the notebook and run the cell using *Shift + Enter*.

The notebook supports six heading sizes, from **Heading 1** (the largest) to **Heading 6** (the smallest).

 The Markdown language also allows the insertion of headings, using the hash (#) symbol. Even though this saves typing, we recommend the use of the Heading 1 to Heading 6 cells. Having the headings in separate cells keeps the structure of the notebook when it is saved. This structure is used by the `nbconvert` utility.

The following table summarizes the types of cells we considered so far:

Cell type	Command mode shortcuts	Use
Code	*Y*	This allows you to edit and write new code to the IPython interpreter. The Default language is Python.
Markdown	*M*	This allows you to write an explanatory text.
Heading 1 to Heading 6	Keys *1* to *6*	This allows you to structure the document
Raw NBConvert	*R*	The content of this cell remains unmodified when the notebook is converted to a different format

IPython magics

Magics are special instructions to the IPython interpreter that perform specialized actions. There are two types of magics:

- **Line-oriented**: This type of magics start with a single percent (%) sign
- **Cell-oriented**: This type of magics start with double percent (%%) signs

We are already familiar with one of the magic command, that is, `%pylab inline`. This particular magic does two of the following things: it imports NumPy and matplotlib, and sets up the notebook for inline plots. To see one of the other options, change the cell to `%pylab`.

Run this cell and then run the cell that produces the plot again. Instead of drawing the graph inline, IPython will now open a new window with the plot as shown in the following screenshot:

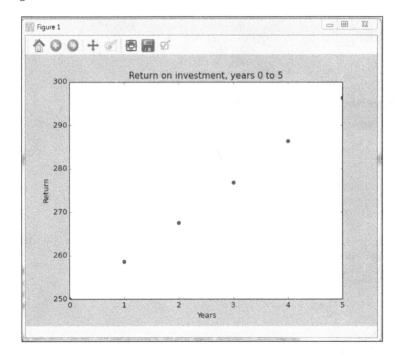

This window is interactive and you can resize the graph, move it, and save it to a file from here.

Another useful magic is `%timeit`, which records the time it takes to run a line of Python code. Run the following code in a new cell in the notebook:

```
%timeit return_on_investment(principal, interest_rate, tvalues)
```

The output will be something like this:

```
100000 loops, best of 3: 3.73 µs per loop
```

To obtain a better estimate, the command is run 10,000 times and the runtime is averaged. This is done three times and the best result is reported.

The `%timeit` magic is also available in the Edit mode. To demonstrate this, run the following command in a cell:

```
principal = 250
interest_rates = [0.0001 * i for i in range(100000)]
tfinal = 10
```

In the next cell, run the following command:

```
%%timeit
returns = []
for r in interest_rates:
    returns.append(return_on_investment(principal, r, tfinal))
```

The preceding code computes a list with the returns for 100,000 different values of the interest rate, but uses plain Python code only. The reported time for this code is displayed in the following output:

```
10 loops, best of 3: 31.6 ms per loop
```

Let's now rewrite the same computation using NumPy arrays. Run the following command in a cell:

```
principal = 250
interest_rates = arange(0, 10, 0.0001)
tfinal = 10
```

In the next cell, run the following command:

```
%%timeit
returns = return_on_investment(principal, interest_rates, tfinal)
```

Now, the runtime is displayed in the following output:

```
100 loops, best of 3: 5.53 ms per loop
```

When comparing the two outputs, we can see the speed gain obtained using `NumPy`.

To list all magics that are available, run the following command in a cell:

```
%lsmagic
```

Once you have the list of all magics, you can inquire about a particular one by running a cell with the magic name appended by a question mark: `%pylab?`.

This will display the information about the `%pylab` magic in a separate window at the bottom of the browser.

Another interesting feature is the capability to run code that is written in other languages. Just to illustrate the possibilities, we'll see how to accelerate the code using Cython, because Cython compiles Python code into C. Let's write a function that computes approximations of areas bounded by a sine curve. Here is how we could define the function in pure Python:

```python
import math
def sin_area(a, b, nintervals):
    dx = (b-a)/nintervals
    sleft = 0.0
    sright = 0.0
    for i in range(nintervals):
        sleft += math.sin(a + i * dx)
        sright += math.sin(a + (i + 1) * dx)
    return dx * (sright + sleft) / 2
```

We will approximate the area by taking the average of the left and right endpoint rules (which is equivalent to the Trapezoidal rule). The code is admittedly inefficient and unpythonic. Notice in particular that we use the Python library version of the `sin()` function, instead of the `NumPy` implementation. The `NumPy` implementation, in this case, actually yields a slower code due to the repeated conversions between lists and arrays.

To run a simple test, execute the following command in a cell:

```
sin_area(0, pi, 10000)
```

We get the following output after running the preceding cell:

```
1.999999835506606
```

The output makes sense, since the actual value of the area is 2. Let's now time the execution using the following command:

```
%timeit sin_area(0, pi, 10000)
```

We will get the following output:

```
100 loops, best of 3: 3.7 ms per loop
```

Let's now implement the same function in Cython. Since the Cython magic is in an extension module, we need to load that module first. We will load the extension module using the following command:

```
%load_ext cythonmagic
```

Now, we will define the Cython function. We will not discuss the syntax in detail, but notice that it is pretty similar to Python (the main difference in this example is that we must declare the variables to specify their C type):

```
%%cython
cimport cython
from libc.math cimport sin


@cython.cdivision(True)
def sin_area_cython(a, b, nintervals):
    cdef double dx, sleft, sright
    cdef int i
    dx = (b-a)/nintervals
    sleft = 0.0
    sright = 0.0
    for i in range(nintervals):
        sleft += sin(a + i * dx)
        sright += sin(a + (i + 1) * dx)
    return dx * (sright + sleft) / 2
```

Test the preceding function using the following command:

```
sin_area_cython(0, pi, 10000)
```

After running the preceding function, we get the same output as earlier:

```
1.9999999835506608
```

Let's now time the function using the following command:

```
%timeit sin_area_cython(0, pi, 10000)
```

The runtime is displayed in the following output:

```
1000 loops, best of 3: 1.12 ms per loop
```

We see that the Cython code runs in about 30 percent of the total time taken by the Python code. It is important to emphasize that this is not the recommended way to speed up this code. A simpler solution would be to use NumPy to vectorize the computation:

```
def sin_area_numpy(a, b, nintervals):
    dx = (b - a) / nintervals
    xvalues = arange(a, b, dx)
    sleft = sum(sin(xvalues))
    sright = sum(sin(xvalues + dx))
    return dx * (sleft + sright) / 2
```

The time after running the preceding code is displayed in the following output:

```
1000 loops, best of 3: 248 µs per loop
```

There is a lesson here; when we try to speed up the code, the first thing to try is to always write it using NumPy arrays, taking the advantage of vectorized functions. If further speedups are needed, we can use specialized libraries such as **Numba** and **NumbaPro** (which will be discussed later in this book) to accelerate the code. In fact, these libraries provide a simpler approach to compile the code into C than using Cython directly.

Interacting with the operating system

Any code with some degree of complexity will interact with the computer's operating system when files must be opened and closed, scripts must be run, or online data must be accessed. Plain Python already has a lot of tools to access these facilities, and IPython and the notebook add another level of functionality and convenience.

Saving the notebook

The notebook is autosaved in periodic intervals. The default interval is 2 minutes, but this can be changed in the configuration files or using the %autosave magic. For example, to change the autosave interval to 5 minutes, run the following command:

```
%autosave 300
```

Notice that the time is entered in seconds. To disable the autosave feature, run the following command:

```
%autosave 0
```

We can also save the notebook using the **File** menu or by clicking on the disk icon on the toolbar. This creates a **checkpoint**. Checkpoints are stored in a hidden folder and can be restored from the **File** menu. Notice that only the latest checkpoint is made available.

Notebooks are saved as plain text files with the `.ipynb` extension, using JSON. JSON is a format widely used for information exchange in web applications, and is documented in `http://www.json.org/`. This makes it easy to exchange notebooks with other people: simply give them the `.ipynb` file, and it can then be copied to the appropriate working directory. The next time the notebook server is opened in that directory, the new notebook will be available (or the directory list can be refreshed from the dashboard). Also, since JSON is in a plain text format, it can be easily versioned.

Converting the notebook to other formats

Notebooks can be converted to other formats using the `nbconvert` utility. This is a command-line utility. So, to use it, open a terminal window in the directory that contains your notebook files.

 Windows users can press *Shift* and right-click on the name of the directory that contains the notebook files and then select **Open command window here**.

Open a shell window and enter the following line:

```
ipython nbconvert "Chapter 2.ipynb"
```

You must, of course, replace `Chapter 2.ipynb` with the name of the file that contains your notebook. The file name must be enclosed by quotes.

The preceding command will convert the notebook to a static HTML page that can be directly placed in a web server.

 An alternative way to publish notebooks on the Web is to use the site `http://nbviewer.ipython.org/`.

It is also possible to create a slideshow with `nbconvert` using the following command:

```
ipython nbconvert "Chapter 2.ipynb" --to slides
```

However, to get a decent presentation, we must first specify its structure in the notebook. To do so, go to the notebook and select **Slide show** on the **Cell** toolbar drop-down list. Then, determine for each cell if it should be a slide, a sub-slide, or a fragment.

To view the slide show, you need to install the `reveal.js` file in the same directory as the web page containing the presentation. You can download this file from `https://github.com/hakimel/reveal.js`. If necessary, rename the directory that contains all the files to `reveal.js`. We are then ready to open the HTML file that contains the presentation.

It is also possible to convert notebooks to LaTeX and PDF. However, this requires the installation of packages not included in Anaconda.

Running shell commands

We can run any shell command from the notebook by starting a cell with an exclamation (!) mark. For example, to obtain a directory listing in Windows, run the following command in a cell:

```
!dir
```

The equivalent command in Linux or OS X is the following:

```
!ls
```

You can enter command lines of any complexity in the cell. For example, the following line would compile the famous "Hello, world!" program every student of C has to try:

```
!cc hello.c -o hello
```

Of course, this will not run correctly in your computer unless you have the C compiler, `cc`, installed and the `hello.c` file with the proper code.

Instead of using shell commands directly, a lot of the same functionality is provided by magic commands. For example, a directory listing (in any operating system) is obtained by running the following command:

```
%ls
```

The following table shows a list of some of the most commonly used magics to interact with the system:

Magic	Purpose
`%cd`	Changes the directory
`%pwd`	Prints the current directory
`%ls`	Lists the current directory contents
`%mkdir`	Creates a new directory
`%rmdir`	Removes a directory
`%echo`	Prints a string
`%alias`	Creates an alias

The `%echo` magic is frequently used to print values of environment variables. For example, to print the contents of the PATH environment variable in Windows, run the following command:

```
%echo %PATH%
```

In Linux or OS X, use the following command:

```
%echo $PATH
```

The `%alias` magic creates an alias for frequently used commands. For example, to define a macro that displays the PATH value in Windows, execute the following command:

```
%alias show_path echo %PATH%
```

In Linux or OS X, use the following command:

```
%alias show_path echo $PATH
```

After the preceding command is defined, we can run the following command to display the path:

```
show_path
```

To make entering commands even easier, a feature called **automagic** allows line-oriented magics to be entered without the `%` symbol (as shown in the preceding command). For example, to create a directory, we can simply enter the following command:

```
mkdir my-directory
```

If we change our mind, we can remove the directory using the following command:

```
rmdir my-directory
```

The automagic feature is controlled by the `%automagic` magic. For example, use the following command to turn automagic off:

```
%automagic off
```

Running scripts, loading data, and saving data

When working with projects of some complexity, it is common to have the need to run scripts written by others. It is also always necessary to load data and save results. In this section, we will describe the facilities that IPython provides for these tasks.

Running Python scripts

The following Python script generates a plot of a solution of the Lorenz equations, a famous example in the theory of chaos. If you are typing the code, do not type it in a cell in the notebook. Instead, use a text editor and save the file with the name `lorenz.py` in the same directory that contains the notebook file. The code is as follows:

```python
import numpy as np
import matplotlib.pyplot as plt
from scipy.integrate import odeint
from mpl_toolkits.mplot3d import Axes3D

def make_lorenz(sigma, r, b):
    def func(statevec, t):
        x, y, z = statevec
        return [ sigma * (y - x),
                 r * x - y - x * z,
                 x * y - b * z ]
    return func

lorenz_eq = make_lorenz(10., 28., 8./3.)

tmax = 50
tdelta = 0.005
tvalues = np.arange(0, tmax, tdelta)
```

```
ic = np.array([0.0, 1.0, 0.0])
sol = odeint(lorenz_eq, ic, tvalues)

x, y, z = np.array(zip(*sol))

fig = plt.figure(figsize=(10,10))
ax = fig.add_subplot(111, projection='3d')
ax.plot(x, y, z, lw=1, color='red')
ax.set_xlabel('$x$')
ax.set_ylabel('$y$')
ax.set_zlabel('$z$')
plt.show()
```

Now, go to the notebook and run a cell using the following command:

`%run lorenz.py`

This will run the script and produce a plot of the solution, as shown in the following figure:

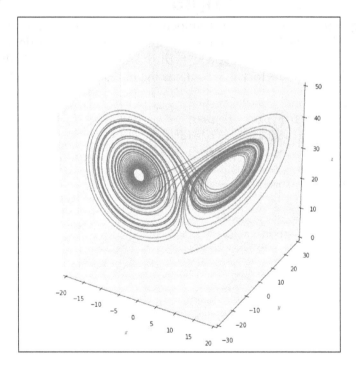

The `%run` magic executes the script in the notebook's namespace so that all global variables, functions, and classes defined in the script are made available in the current notebook.

It is also possible to use the `%load` magic for the same purpose:

```
%load lorenz.py
```

The difference is that `%load` does not immediately run the script, but places its code in a cell. It can then be run from the cell it was inserted in. A slightly annoying behavior of the `%load` magic is that it inserts a new cell with the script code even if there already is one from a previous use of `%load`. The notebook has no way of knowing if the user wants to overwrite the code in the existing cell, so this is the safest behavior. However, unwanted code must be deleted manually.

The `%load` magic also allows code to be loaded directly from the web by providing a URL as input:

```
%load http://matplotlib.org/mpl_examples/pylab_examples/boxplot_demo2.py
```

This will load the code for a box plot example from the matplotlib site to a cell. To display the image, the script must be run in the cell.

Running scripts in other languages

We can also run scripts written in other languages directly in the notebook. The following table contains some of the supported languages:

Cell magic	Language
`%%HTML` or `%%html`	HTML
`%%SVG` or `%%svg`	**Scaled Vector Graphics Language (SVGL)**
`%%bash`	The Bash scripting language, which is available in Unix-like systems such as Ubuntu and Mac OS X
`%%cmd`	MS Windows command-line language
`%%javascript`	JavaScript
`%%latex`	LaTeX, the scientific-oriented document preparation language
`%%perl`	The PERL scripting language
`%%powershell`	The MS Windows PowerShell language
`%%python2` or `%%python3`	Run a script written in a version of Python different than the one the notebook is running
`%%ruby`	The Ruby scripting language

Now, let's see some examples of scripts in some of these languages. Run the following code in a cell:

```
%%SVG
<svg width="400" height="300">
    <circle  cx="200" cy="150" r="100"
        style="fill:Wheat; stroke:SteelBlue; stroke-width:5;"/>
    <line x1="10" y1="10" x2="250" y2="85"
        style="stroke:SlateBlue; stroke-width:4"/>
    <polyline points="20,30 50,70 100,25 200,120"
        style="stroke:orange; stroke-width:3;
                fill:olive; opacity:0.65;"/>
    <rect x="30" y="150" width="120" height="75"
        style="stroke:Navy; stroke-width:4; fill:LightSkyBlue;"/>
    <ellipse cx="310" cy="220" rx="55" ry="75"
        style="stroke:DarkSlateBlue; stroke-width:4;
                fill:DarkOrange; fill-opacity:0.45;"/>
    <polygon points="50,50 15,100 75,200 45,100"
        style="stroke:DarkTurquoise; stroke-width:5; fill:Beige;"/>
</svg>
```

This displays a graphic composition with basic shapes, described using SVG. SVG is an HTML standard, so this code will run in modern browsers that support the standard.

To illustrate the use of JavaScript, let's first define (in a computation cell) an HTML element that can be easily accessed:

```
%%html
<h1 id="hellodisplay">Hello, world!</h1>
```

Run this cell. The message "Hello, world!" in the size h1 is displayed. Then enter the following commands in another cell:

```
%%javascript
element = document.getElementById("hellodisplay")
element.style.color = 'blue'
```

When the second cell is run, the color of the text of the "Hello, world!" message changes from black to blue.

The notebook can actually run any scripting language that is installed in your system. This is done using the `%%script` cell magic. As an example, let's run some code in the **Julia** scripting language. Julia is a new language for technical computing and can be downloaded from `http://julialang.org/`. The following example assumes that Julia is installed and can be accessed with the `julia` command (this requires that the executable for the language interpreter is in the operating system's path). Enter the following code in a cell and run it:

```
%%script julia
function factorial(n::Int)
    fact = 1
    for k=1:n
      fact *= k
    end
    fact
end

println(factorial(10))
```

The preceding code defines a function (written in `julia`) that computes the factorial of an integer, and then prints the factorial of 10. The following output is produced:

```
factorial (generic function with 1 method)
3628800
```

The first line is a message from the `julia` interpreter and the second is the factorial of 10.

Loading and saving data

The manner in which data is loaded or saved is dependent on both the nature of the data and the format expected by the application that is using the data. Since it's impossible to account for all combinations of data structure and application, we will only cover the most basic methods of loading and saving data using `NumPy` in this section. The recommended way to load and save structured data in Python is to use specialized libraries that have been optimized for each particular data type. When working with tabular data, for example, we can use **pandas**, as described in *Chapter 4, Handling Data with pandas*.

A single array can be saved with a call to the `save()` function of NumPy. Here is an example:

```
A = rand(5, 10)
print A
save('random_array.npy', A)
```

This code generates an array of random values with five rows and 10 columns, prints it, and then saves it to a file named `random_array.npy`. The `.npy` format is specific for NumPy arrays. Let's now delete the variable containing the array using the following command:

```
del A
A
```

Running a cell with the preceding commands will produce an error, since we request the variable A to be displayed after it has been deleted. To restore the array, run the following command in a cell:

```
A = load('random_array.npy')
A
```

It is also possible to save several arrays to a single compressed file, as shown in the following example:

```
xvalues = arange(0.0, 10.0, 0.5)
xsquares = xvalues ** 2
print xvalues
print xsquares
savez('values_and_squares.npz', values=xvalues, squares=xsquares)
```

Notice how keyword arguments are given to specify names for the saved arrays in disk. The arrays are now saved to a file in the `.npz` format. The data can be recovered from disk using the `load()` function, which can read files in both formats used by NumPy:

```
my_data = load('values_and_squares.npz')
```

If the file passed to `load()` is of the `.npz` type, the returned value is an object of the `NpzFile` type. This object does not read the data immediately. Reading is delayed to the point where the data is required. To figure out which arrays are stored in the file, execute the following command in a cell:

```
my_data.files
```

In our example, the preceding command produces the following output:

```
['squares', 'values']
```

To assign the arrays to variables, use the Python dictionary access notation as follows:

```
xvalues = my_data['values']
xsquares = my_data['squares']
plot(xvalues, xsquares)
```

The preceding code produces the plot of half of a parabola:

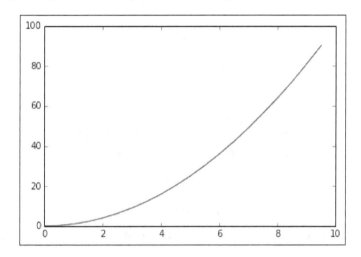

The rich display system

In an exciting development, recent versions of IPython include the capability to display images, video, sound, and other media directly in the notebook. The classes that support the display system are in the `IPython.display` module. In this section, we will discuss some of the supported formats.

Images and YouTube videos

Images can be loaded either from the local filesystem or from the web. To display the image contained in the `character.png` file, for example, run the following command in a cell:

```
from IPython.display import Image
Image('character.png')
```

It is also possible to store the image in a variable to be displayed at a later time:

```
img = Image('character.png')
```

The `character.png` file can be downloaded from the web page of this book.

To display the image, we can use either `img` or `display(img)`. The following image is displayed:

To load an image from the Web, simply give its URL as an argument:

```
Image('http://www.imagesource.com/Doc/IS0/Media/TR5/7/7/f/4/IS09A9H4K.
jpg')
```

The preceding command line loads the image of a flower:

By default, images are embedded in the notebook so that they can be viewed offline. To insert a link to the image, use the following command:

```
Image('http://www.imagesource.com/Doc/IS0/Media/TR5/7/7/f/4/IS09A9H4K.
jpg', embed=False)
```

The image will be displayed as shown in the preceding example, but this time only a link to the image is inserted in the notebook. This results in a smaller size for the notebook file, but there is a caveat! If the image is changed online, the change will be reflected in the notebook.

It is also very easy to embed video directly from YouTube. The following code displays a beautiful animation of the Mandelbrot set:

```
from IPython.display import YouTubeVideo
YouTubeVideo('G_GBwuYuOOs')
```

HTML

To finish this section, we present an extended example using IPython's capability to display HTML. The goal of the example is to build and display an HTML table of mathematical curves. We start by generating the plots and saving them to disk:

```
%matplotlib
xvalues = linspace(-pi,pi,200)
fcts = [('sin', sin), ('cos', cos), ('exp', exp)]
for fctname, fct in fcts:
    yvalues = fct(xvalues)
    fig=figure()
    ax = fig.add_subplot(1,1,1)
    ax.plot(xvalues, yvalues, color='red')
    ax.set_xlabel('$x$')
    strname = '$\\%s(x)$' % fctname
    ax.set_ylabel(strname)
    fig.savefig(fctname + '.png')
```

The cell starts with the `%matplotlib` magic with no arguments, since we don't want the graphics to be inserted online (they will still be generated in an external viewer). We then define the `fcts` list holding the curves we want to plot. Each curve is specified by a tuple with two elements: the name of a function and the actual object representing the function. Then, the plots are generated in a loop. The Python code here is somewhat more complex than what we have seen so far, and the `matplotlib` functions used will be explained in detail in the next chapter. For now, just notice the call at the end of the cell:

```
fig.savefig(fctname + '.png')
```

The preceding command saves the figure file to the disk, using the `.png` format.

Next, we generate the HTML to create the table and store it in the `html_string` variable as follows:

```
html_string = '<table style="padding:20px">\n'
for fctname, fct in fcts:
    strname = strname = '$\\%s(x)$' % fctname
    filename = fctname + '.png'
    html_string += '<tr>\n'
    html_string += '<td style="width:80px;">%s</td>\n' % strname
    html_string += '<td style="width:500px;">'
    html_string += '<img src="%s">' % filename
    html_string += '</td>\n'
    html_string += '</tr>\n'
    html_string += '</table>\n'
```

The HTML code is generated one piece at a time. We start by adding the `<table>` element in the first line of the cell. Then, in the loop, we generate one row of the table per iteration. To make the code more readable, we add only one HTML element in each line of code.

We can then print the HTML we generated to check if it is correct:

```
print html_string
```

The preceding command produces the following output:

```
<table style="padding:20px">
<tr>
<td style="width:80px;">$\sin(x)$</td>
<td style="width:500px;"><img src="sin.png"></td>
</tr>
<tr>
<td style="width:80px;">$\cos(x)$</td>
<td style="width:500px;"><img src="cos.png"></td>
</tr>
<tr>
<td style="width:80px;">$\exp(x)$</td>
<td style="width:500px;"><img src="exp.png"></td>
</tr>
</table>
```

This seems to be correct, so we are ready to render the HTML:

```
from IPython.display import HTML
HTML(html_string)
```

If all is correct, the following table of curves will be displayed:

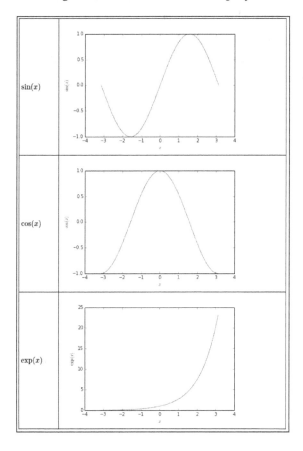

At the end of the example, don't forget to run the following command to restore the inline graphics:

```
%matplotlib inline
```

The IPython HTML display object is extremely powerful, as shown in the preceding example. HTML5-rich media, such as sound and video, can also be embedded; although, the support for all formats currently varies from browser to browser.

Summary

In this chapter, we went through a comprehensive tour of the IPython Notebook Interface. We covered features that are used daily when working with the notebook, such as navigation, magics, interacting with the operating system, running scripts, and loading and saving data. We finished with a discussion of how to display richly formatted data in the notebook.

In the next chapter, you will learn how to use the `matplotlib` library to produce presentation-quality scientific graphs and data displays, with an emphasis on interactive graphs.

3
Graphics with matplotlib

This chapter explores matplotlib, an IPython library for production of publication-quality graphs. In this chapter, the following topics will be discussed:

- Two-dimensional plots using the `plot` function and setting up line widths, colors, and styles
- Plot configuration and annotation
- Three-dimensional plots
- Animations

Being an IPython library, matplotlib consists of a hierarchy of classes, and it is possible to code using it in the usual object-oriented style. However, matplotlib also supports an **interactive** mode. In this mode, the graphs are constructed step-by-step, thus adding and configuring each component at a time. We lay emphasis on the second approach since it is designed for the rapid production of graphs. The object-oriented style will be explained whenever it is needed or leads to better results.

The sense in which the word *interactive* is used in this context is somewhat different from what is understood today. Graphs produced by matplotlib are not interactive in the sense that the user can manipulate the graphs once they have been rendered in the notebook. Instead, the terminology comes from the time when matplotlib was used mostly in command-line mode, and each new line of code modified the existing plots. Curiously, the software that was the original inspiration for matplotlib still uses a command line-based interface.

The plot function

The `plot()` function is the workhorse of the matplotlib library. In this section, we will explore the line-plotting and formatting capabilities included in this function.

To make things a bit more concrete, let's consider the formula for **logistic growth**, as follows:

$$N(t) = \frac{a}{b + ce^{-rt}}$$

This model is frequently used to represent growth that shows an initial exponential phase, and then is eventually limited by some factor. The examples are the population in an environment with limited resources and new products and/or technological innovations, which initially attract a small and quickly growing market but eventually reach a saturation point.

A common strategy to understand a mathematical model is to investigate how it changes as the parameters defining it are modified. Let's say, we want to see what happens to the shape of the curve when the parameter b changes.

To be able to do what we want more efficiently, we are going to use a **function factory**. This way, we can quickly create logistic models with arbitrary values for r, a, b, and c. Run the following code in a cell:

```
def make_logistic(r, a, b, c):
    def f_logistic(t):
        return a / (b + c * exp(-r * t))
    return f_logistic
```

The function factory pattern takes advantage of the fact that functions are **first-class objects** in Python. This means that functions can be treated as regular objects: they can be assigned to variables, stored in lists in dictionaries, and play the role of arguments and/or return values in other functions.

In our example, we define the `make_logistic()` function, whose output is itself a Python function. Notice how the `f_logistic()` function is defined *inside* the body of `make_logistic()` and then returned in the last line.

Let's now use the function factory to create three functions representing logistic curves, as follows:

```
r = 0.15
a = 20.0
c = 15.0
```

```
b1, b2, b3 = 2.0, 3.0, 4.0
logistic1 = make_logistic(r, a, b1, c)
logistic2 = make_logistic(r, a, b2, c)
logistic3 = make_logistic(r, a, b3, c)
```

In the preceding code, we first fix the values of r, a, and c, and define three logistic curves for different values of b. The important point to notice is that `logistic1`, `logistic2`, and `logistic3` are functions. So, for example, we can use `logistic1(2.5)` to compute the value of the first logistic curve at the time 2.5.

We can now plot the functions using the following code:

```
tmax = 40
tvalues = linspace(0, tmax, 300)
plot(tvalues, logistic1(tvalues))
plot(tvalues, logistic2(tvalues))
plot(tvalues, logistic3(tvalues))
```

The first line in the preceding code sets the maximum time value, `tmax`, to be `40`. Then, we define the set of times at which we want the functions evaluated with the assignment, as follows:

```
tvalues = linspace(0, tmax, 300)
```

The `linspace()` function is very convenient to generate points for plotting. The preceding code creates an array of 300 equally spaced points in the interval from `0` to `tmax`. Note that, contrary to other functions, such as `range()` and `arange()`, the right endpoint of the interval is included by default. (To exclude the right endpoint, use the `endpoint=False` option.)

After defining the array of time values, the `plot()` function is called to graph the curves. In its most basic form, it plots a single curve in a default color and line style. In this usage, the two arguments are two arrays. The first array gives the horizontal coordinates of the points being plotted, and the second array gives the vertical coordinates. A typical example will be the following function call:

```
plot(x,y)
```

The variables x and y must refer to NumPy arrays (or any Python iterable values that can be converted into an array) and must have the same dimensions. The points plotted have coordinates as follows:

```
x[0], y[0]
x[1], y[1]
x[2], y[2]
...
```

The preceding command will produce the following plot, displaying the three logistic curves:

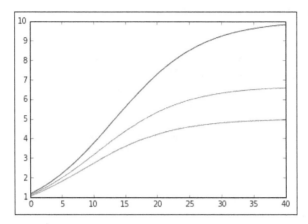

You may have noticed that before the graph is displayed, there is a line of text output that looks like the following:

```
[<matplotlib.lines.Line2D at 0x7b57c50>]
```

This is the return value of the last call to the `plot()` function, which is a list (or with a single element) of objects of the `Line2D` type. One way to prevent the output from being shown is to enter `None` as the last row in the cell. Alternatively, we can assign the return value of the last call in the cell to a dummy variable:

```
_dummy_ = plot(tvalues, logistic3(tvalues))
```

The `plot()` function supports plotting several curves in the same function call. We need to change the contents of the cell that are shown in the following code and run it again:

```
tmax = 40
tvalues = linspace(0, tmax, 300)
plot(tvalues, logistic1(tvalues),
     tvalues, logistic2(tvalues),
     tvalues, logistic3(tvalues))
```

This form saves some typing but turns out to be a little less flexible when it comes to customizing line options. Notice that the text output produced now is a list with three elements:

```
[<matplotlib.lines.Line2D at 0x9bb6cc0>,
 <matplotlib.lines.Line2D at 0x9bb6ef0>,
 <matplotlib.lines.Line2D at 0x9bb9518>]
```

This output can be useful in some instances. For now, we will stick with using one call to `plot()` for each curve, since it produces code that is clearer and more flexible.

Let's now change the line options in the plot and set the plot bounds. Change the contents of the cell to read as follows:

```
plot(tvalues, logistic1(tvalues),
     linewidth=1.5, color='DarkGreen', linestyle='-')
plot(tvalues, logistic2(tvalues),
     linewidth=2.0, color='#8B0000', linestyle=':')
plot(tvalues, logistic3(tvalues),
     linewidth=3.5, color=(0.0, 0.0, 0.5), linestyle='--')
axis([0, tmax, 0, 11.])
None
```

Running the preceding command lines will produce the following plots:

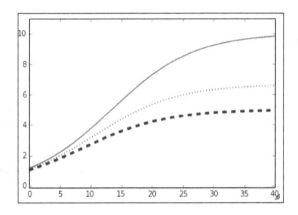

The options set in the preceding code are as follows:

- The first curve is plotted with a line width of `1.5`, with the HTML color of `DarkGreen`, and a filled-line style

- The second curve is plotted with a line width of `2.0`, colored with the RGB value given by the hexadecimal string `#8B0000`, and a dotted-line style

- The third curve is plotted with a line width of `3.0`, colored with the RGB components, `(0.0, 0.0, 0.5)`, and a dashed-line style

Notice that there are different ways of specifying a fixed color: a HTML color name, a hexadecimal string, or a tuple of floating-point values. In the last case, the entries in the tuple represent the intensity of the red, green, and blue colors, respectively, and must be floating-point values between `0.0` and `1.0`. A complete list of HTML name colors can be found at `http://www.w3schools.com/html/html_colornames.asp`.

Line styles are specified by a symbolic string. The allowed values are shown in the following table:

Symbol string	Line style
'-'	Solid (the default)
'- -'	Dashed
':'	Dotted
'-.'	Dash-dot
'None', ' ', or ''	Not displayed

After the calls to `plot()`, we set the graph bounds with the function call:

```
axis([0, tmax, 0, 11.])
```

The argument to `axis()` is a four-element list that specifies, in this order, the maximum and minimum values of the horizontal coordinates, and the maximum and minimum values of the vertical coordinates.

It may seem non-intuitive that the bounds for the variables are set after the plots are drawn. In the interactive mode, matplotlib remembers the state of the graph being constructed, and graphics objects are updated in the background after each command is issued. The graph is only rendered when all computations in the cell are done so that all previously specified options take effect. Note that starting a new cell clears all the graph data. This interactive behavior is part of the `matplotlib.pyplot` module, which is one of the components imported by `pylab`.

Besides drawing a line connecting the data points, it is also possible to draw markers at specified points. Change the graphing commands indicated in the following code snippet, and then run the cell again:

```
plot(tvalues, logistic1(tvalues),
     linewidth=1.5, color='DarkGreen', linestyle='-',
     marker='o', markevery=50, markerfacecolor='GreenYellow',
     markersize=10.0)
plot(tvalues, logistic2(tvalues),
     linewidth=2.0, color='#8B0000', linestyle=':',
     marker='s', markevery=50, markerfacecolor='Salmon',
     markersize=10.0)
plot(tvalues, logistic3(tvalues),
     linewidth=2.0, color=(0.0, 0.0, 0.5), linestyle='--',
     marker = '*', markevery=50, markerfacecolor='SkyBlue',
     markersize=12.0)
axis([0, tmax, 0, 11.])
None
```

Now, the graph will look as shown in the following figure:

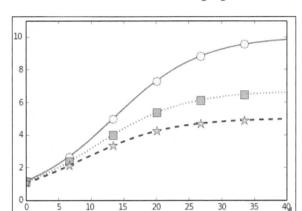

The only difference from the previous code is that now we added options to draw markers. The following are the options we use:

- The `marker` option specifies the shape of the marker. Shapes are given as symbolic strings. In the preceding examples, we use `'o'` for a circular marker, `'s'` for a square, and `'*'` for a star. A complete list of available markers can be found at `http://matplotlib.org/api/markers_api.html#module-matplotlib.markers`.

- The `markevery` option specifies a stride within the data points for the placement of markers. In our example, we place a marker after every 50 data points.

- The `markercolor` option specifies the color of the marker.

- The `markersize` option specifies the size of the marker. The size is given in pixels.

There are a large number of other options that can be applied to lines in matplotlib. A complete list is available at `http://matplotlib.org/api/artist_api.html#module-matplotlib.lines`.

Adding a title, labels, and a legend

The next step is to add a title and labels for the axes. Just before the `None` line, add the following three lines of code to the cell that creates the graph:

```
title('Logistic growth: a={:5.2f}, c={:5.2f}, r={:5.2f}'.format(a, c, r))
xlabel('$t$')
ylabel('$N(t)=a/(b+ce^{-rt})$')
```

In the first line, we call the `title()` function to set the title of the plot. The argument can be any Python string. In our example, we use a formatted string:

```
title('Logistic growth: a={:5.2f}, b={:5.2f}, r={:5.2f}'.format(a, c, r))
```

We use the `format()` method of the string class. The formats are placed between braces, as in `{:5.2f}`, which specifies a floating-point format with five spaces and two digits of precision. Each of the format specifiers is then associated sequentially with one of the data arguments of the method. Some of the details of string formatting are covered in *Appendix B, A Brief Review of Python*, and the full documentation is available at https://docs.python.org/2/library/string.html.

The axis labels are set in the calls:

```
xlabel('$t$')
```

```
ylabel('$N(t)=a/(b+ce^{-rt})$')
```

As in the `title()` functions, the `xlabel()` and `ylabel()` functions accept any Python string. Note that in the `'$t$'` and `'$N(t)=a/(b+ce^{-rt}$'` strings, we use LaTeX to format the mathematical formulas. This is indicated by the dollar signs, `$...$`, in the string.

After the addition of a title and labels, our graph looks like the following:

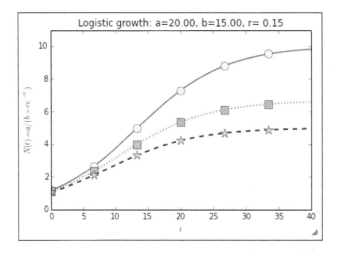

Next, we need a way to identify each of the curves in the picture. One way to do that is to use a `legend`, which is indicated as follows:

```
legend(['b={:5.2f}'.format(b1),
        'b={:5.2f}'.format(b2),
        'b={:5.2f}'.format(b3)])
```

The `legend()` function accepts a list of strings. Each string is associated with a curve in the order they are added to the plot. Notice that we are again using formatted strings.

Unfortunately, the preceding code does not produce great results. The legend, by default, is placed in the top-right corner of the plot, which, in this case, hides part of the graph. This is easily fixed using the `loc` option in the `legend` function, as shown in the following code:

```
legend(['b={:5.2f}'.format(b1),
        'b={:5.2f}'.format(b2),
        'b={:5.2f}'.format(b3)], loc='upper left')
```

Running this code, we obtain the final version of our logistic growth plot, as follows:

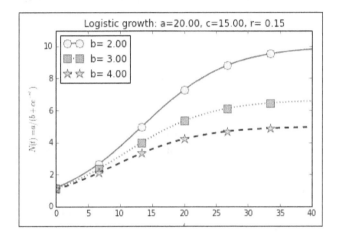

The legend location can be any of the strings: `'best'`, `'upper right'`, `'upper left'`, `'lower left'`, `'lower right'`, `'right'`, `'center left'`, `'center right'`, `'lower center'`, `'upper center'`, and `'center'`. It is also possible to specify the location of the legend precisely with the `bbox_to_anchor` option. To see how this works, modify the code for the legend as follows:

```
legend(['b={:5.2f}'.format(b1),
        'b={:5.2f}'.format(b2),
        'b={:5.2f}'.format(b3)],  bbox_to_anchor=(0.9,0.35))
```

Notice that the `bbox_to_anchor` option, by default, uses a coordinate system that is not the same as the one we specified for the plot. The x and y coordinates of the box in the preceding example are interpreted as a fraction of the width and height, respectively, of the whole figure. A little trial-and-error is necessary to place the legend box precisely where we want it. Note that the legend box can be placed outside the plot area. For example, try the coordinates `(1.32,1.02)`.

The `legend()` function is quite flexible and has quite a few other options that are documented at `http://matplotlib.org/api/pyplot_api.html#matplotlib.pyplot.legend`.

Text and annotations

In this subsection, we will show how to add annotations to plots in matplotlib. We will build a plot demonstrating the fact that the tangent to a curve must be horizontal at the highest and lowest points. We start by defining the function associated with the curve and the set of values at which we want the curve to be plotted, which is shown in the following code:

```
f = lambda x:   (x**3 - 6*x**2 + 9*x + 3) / (1 + 0.25*x**2)
xvalues = linspace(0, 5, 200)
```

The first line in the preceding code uses a lambda expression to define the `f()` function. We use this approach here because the formula for the function is a simple, one-line expression. The general form of a lambda expression is as follows:

```
lambda <arguments> : <return expression>
```

This expression by itself creates an anonymous function that can be used in any place that a function object is expected. Note that the return value must be a single expression and cannot contain any statements.

The formula for the function may seem unusual, but it was chosen by trial-and-error and a little bit of calculus so that it produces a nice graph in the interval from 0 to 5. The `xvalues` array is defined to contain 200 equally spaced points on this interval.

Let's create an initial plot of our curve, as shown in the following code:

```
plot(xvalues, f(xvalues), lw=2, color='FireBrick')
axis([0, 5, -1, 8])
grid()
xlabel('$x$')
ylabel('$f(x)$')
title('Extreme values of a function')
None # Prevent text output
```

Most of the code in this segment is explained in the previous section. The only new bit is that we use the `grid()` function to draw a grid. Used with no arguments, the grid coincides with the tick marks on the plot. As everything else in matplotlib, grids are highly customizable. Check the documentation at `http://matplotlib.org/1.3.1/api/pyplot_api.html#matplotlib.pyplot.grid`.

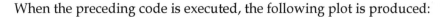

When the preceding code is executed, the following plot is produced:

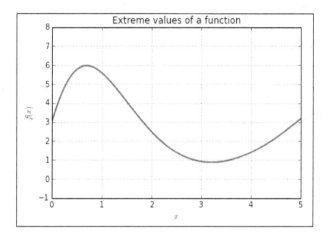

Note that the curve has a highest point (*maximum*) and a lowest point (*minimum*). These are collectively called the *extreme values* of the function (on the displayed interval, this function actually grows without bounds as *x* becomes large). We would like to locate these on the plot with annotations. We will first store the relevant points as follows:

```
x_min = 3.213
f_min = f(x_min)
x_max = 0.698
f_max = f(x_max)
p_min = array([x_min, f_min])
p_max = array([x_max, f_max])
print p_min
print p_max
```

The variables, x_min and f_min, are defined to be (approximately) the coordinates of the lowest point in the graph. Analogously, x_max and f_max represent the highest point. Don't be concerned with how these points were found. For the purposes of graphing, even a rough approximation by trial-and-error would suffice. In *Chapter 5, Advanced Computing with SciPy, Numba, and NumbaPro*, we will see how to solve this kind of problem accurately via SciPy. Now, add the following code to the cell that draws the plot, right below the title() command, as shown in the following code:

```
arrow_props = dict(facecolor='DimGray', width=3, shrink=0.05,
            headwidth=7)
delta = array([0.1, 0.1])
offset = array([1.0, .85])
```

```
annotate('Maximum', xy=p_max+delta, xytext=p_max+offset,
        arrowprops=arrow_props, verticalalignment='bottom',
        horizontalalignment='left', fontsize=13)
annotate('Minimum', xy=p_min-delta, xytext=p_min-offset,
        arrowprops=arrow_props, verticalalignment='top',
        horizontalalignment='right', fontsize=13)
```

Run the cell to produce the plot shown in the following diagram:

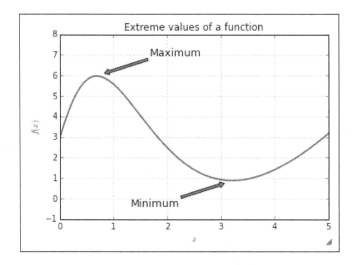

In the code, start by assigning the variables `arrow_props`, `delta`, and `offset`, which will be used to set the arguments in the calls to `annotate()`. The `annotate()` function adds a textual annotation to the graph with an optional arrow indicating the point being annotated. The first argument of the function is the text of the annotation. The next two arguments give the locations of the arrow and the text:

- `xy`: This is the point being annotated and will correspond to the tip of the arrow. We want this to be the maximum/minimum points, `p_min` and `p_max`, but we add/subtract the `delta` vector so that the tip is a bit removed from the actual point.

- `xytext`: This is the point where the text will be placed as well as the base of the arrow. We specify this as offsets from `p_min` and `p_max` using the `offset` vector.

All other arguments of `annotate()` are formatting options:

- `arrowprops`: This is a Python dictionary containing the arrow properties. We predefine the dictionary, `arrow_props`, and use it here. Arrows can be quite sophisticated in matplotlib, and you are directed to the documentation for details.
- `verticalalignment` and `horizontalalignment`: These specify how the arrow should be aligned with the text.
- `fontsize`: This signifies the size of the text. Text is also highly configurable, and the reader is directed to the documentation for details.

The `annotate()` function has a huge number of options; for complete details of what is available, users should consult the documentation at http://matplotlib. org/1.3.1/api/pyplot_api.html#matplotlib.pyplot.annotate for the full details.

We now want to add a comment for what is being demonstrated by the plot by adding an explanatory textbox. Add the following code to the cell right after the calls to `annotate()`:

```
bbox_props = dict(boxstyle='round', lw=2, fc='Beige')
text(2, 6, 'Maximum and minimum points\nhave horizontal tangents',
    bbox=bbox_props, fontsize=12, verticalalignment='top')
```

The `text()` function is used to place text at an arbitrary position of the plot. The first two arguments are the position of the textbox, and the third argument is a string containing the text to be displayed. Notice the use of `'\n'` to indicate a line break. The other arguments are configuration options. The `bbox` argument is a dictionary with the options for the box. If omitted, the text will be displayed without any surrounding box. In the example code, the box is a rectangle with rounded corners, with a border width of 2 pixels and the face color, beige.

As a final detail, let's add the tangent lines at the extreme points. Add the following code:

```
plot([x_min-0.75, x_min+0.75], [f_min, f_min],
    color='RoyalBlue', lw=3)
plot([x_max-0.75, x_max+0.75], [f_max, f_max],
    color='RoyalBlue', lw=3)
```

Since the tangents are segments of straight lines, we simply give the coordinates of the endpoints. The reason to add the code for the tangents at the top of the cell is that this causes them to be plotted first so that the graph of the function is drawn at the top of the tangents. This is the final result:

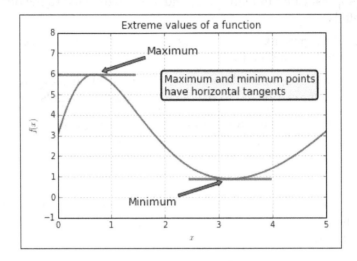

The examples we have seen so far only scratch the surface of what is possible with matplotlib. The reader should read the matplotlib documentation for more examples.

Three-dimensional plots

In this section, we present methods to display three-dimensional plots, that is, plots of mathematical objects in space. Examples include surfaces and lines that are not confined to a plate.

matplotlib has excellent support for three-dimensional plots. In this section, we will present an example of a surface plot and corresponding contour plot. The types of plot available in the three-dimensional library include wireframe plots, line plots, scatterplots, triangulated surface plots, polygon plots, and several others. The following link will help you to understand the types of plots that are not treated here: `http://matplotlib.org/1.3.1/mpl_toolkits/mplot3d/tutorial.html#mplot3d-tutorial`

Before we start, we need to import the three-dimensional library objects we need using the following command line:

```
from mpl_toolkits.mplot3d import axes3d
```

Now, let's draw our surface plot by running the following code in a cell:

```
def dist(x, y):
    return sqrt(x**2 + y**2)
def fsurface(x, y):
    d = sqrt(x**2 + y**2)
    c = 5.0
    r = 7.5
    return c - (d**4 - r * d**2)

xybound = 2.5
fig = figure(figsize=(8,8))
ax = subplot(1, 1, 1, projection='3d')
X = linspace(-xybound, xybound, 25)
Y = linspace(-xybound, xybound, 25)
X, Y = meshgrid(X, Y)
Z = fsurface(X,Y)
ax.plot_surface(X, Y, Z, rstride=1, cstride=1, cmap=cm.coolwarm,
                antialiased=True, linewidth=0.2)
ax.set_xlabel(r'$x$')
ax.set_ylabel(r'$y$')
ax.set_zlabel(r'$f(x,y)$')
None #Prevent text output
```

We start by specifying the `fsurface()` function, which defines the surface. The details of the function definition are not relevant; we will just note that this is a surface of revolution that has a dip at the center, surrounded by a ridge. We then start setting up the figure with the following lines of code:

```
fig = figure(figsize=(8,8))
ax = subplot(1, 1, 1, projection='3d')
```

This time, we specifically construct the `Figure` object because we want to specify its size explicitly. The size here is defined as an 8 x 8 inch square, but this is not quite accurate since the actual size of the figure will depend on the resolution of the display and the magnification factor of the browser. We then create a subplot and set its projection type to `'3d'`. The `subplot()` function will be treated with more detail later in this section.

Next, we will define the grid of points where the function is computed:

```
xybound = 2.5
x = linspace(-xybound, xybound, 25)
y = linspace(-xybound, xybound, 25)
X, Y = meshgrid(x, y)
```

The most important point here is the use of the meshgrid() function, which is a part of the NumPy package. This function takes two one-dimensional arrays, with *x* and *y* values and computes two matrices that define the corresponding grid of points on the plane. To understand how this works, run the following code:

```
xx = [1,2,3]
yy = [4,5,6]
XX, YY = meshgrid(xx, yy)
print XX
print YY
```

The two matrices produced, XX and YY, are as follows:

- The XX matrix:

```
[[1 2 3]
 [1 2 3]
 [1 2 3]]
```

- The YY matrix:

```
[[4 4 4]
 [5 5 5]
 [6 6 6]]
```

Note that, if we take the elements of XX and the corresponding entries in YY, we get the set of points (1,4), (1,5), (1,6), (2,4),..., (3,5), (3,6), which are on a regularly spaced grid on the plane.

We are now ready to call the function that computes the surface and plot it:

```
Z = fsurface(X,Y)
ax.plot_surface(X, Y, Z, rstride=1, cstride=1, cmap=cm.coolwarm,
                antialiased=True, linewidth=0.2)
ax.set_xlabel(r'$x$')
ax.set_ylabel(r'$y$')
ax.set_zlabel(r'$f(x,y)$')
```

The first line computes the z array, containing the *z* coordinates of the surface. This call makes heavy use of a feature of NumPy called **broadcasting** in the background. This is a set of rules that tells us how NumPy deals with operations for arrays with different sizes. For more information, see http://docs.scipy.org/doc/numpy/user/basics.broadcasting.html.

The next step is to call the `plot_surface()` method, which does the actual plotting. The first three arguments define the data being plotted, that is, the arrays X, Y, and Z. The `cstride` and `rstride` options can be used to skip points in the data arrays. Set these to values greater than 1 to skip points in the grid, in the event the data set is too large.

We are using a **colormap** feature specified by the `cmap=cm.coolwarm` option. The colormap feature tells matplotlib how to assign a color to each height in the plot. A large number of built-in colormaps are available. To see a complete list, run the following lines of code in a cell:

```
for key, value in cm.__dict__.items():
    if isinstance(value, matplotlib.colors.Colormap):
        print key
```

Note that three-dimensional surface plots are, by default, not antialiased, so we set the `antialiased=True` option in the code to produce a better image.

Let's now add a contour plot to the graph. We want the three-dimensional surface plot and the contour graph to appear side-by-side. To achieve that, modify the code in the cell to the following:

```
fig = figure(figsize(20,8))
ax1 = subplot(1, 2, 1, projection='3d')
X = linspace(-xybound, xybound, 100)
Y = linspace(-xybound, xybound, 100)
X, Y = np.meshgrid(X, Y)
Z = fsurface(X,Y)
ax1.plot_surface(X, Y, Z, rstride=5, cstride=5, cmap=cm.coolwarm,
                 antialiased=True, linewidth=0.2)
ax1.set_xlabel(r'$x$')
ax1.set_ylabel(r'$y$')
ax1.set_zlabel(r'$f(x,y)$')
ax1.set_title('A surface plot', fontsize=18)
ax2 = subplot(1, 2, 2)
ax2.set_aspect('equal')
levels = arange(5, 20, 2.5)
cs = ax2.contour(X, Y, Z,
            levels,
            cmap=cm.Reds,
            linewidths=1.5)
cs.clabel(levels[1::2], fontsize=12)
ax2.set_title('Contour Plot', fontsize=18)
```

The result of running the code is shown in the following figure:

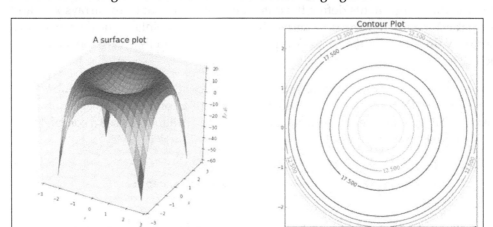

Let's first concentrate on the contours() method. The first argument, levels, specifies the values (heights) for which the contours are plotted. This argument can be left out, and matplotlib will try to choose the heights in a way that makes sense. The other arguments are options for how to display the contours. We specify the colormap and line width in this example.

The clabel() method adds labels to the contours. The first argument, levels[1::2], specifies that every second contour is to be labeled.

Note the code that is used to place two axes in the same figure. The axes are defined by the following command lines:

```
ax1 = subplot(1, 2, 1, projection='3d')
ax2 = subplot(1, 2, 2)
```

The general form of the subplot() function is as follows:

```
subplot(nrows, ncols, axis_position, **kwargs)
```

This specifies an Axes object in an array with nrows rows and ncols columns. The position of the axis is an integer from 1 to nrows*ncols. The following figure illustrates how the axes are numbered in the case of a 3 x 2 array:

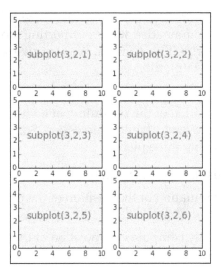

The preceding image was generated with the help of the following command lines:

```
fig = figure(figsize=(5,6))
nrows = 3
ncols = 2
for i in range(nrows*ncols):
    ax = subplot(nrows, ncols, i+1, axisbg='Bisque')
    axis([0,10,0,5])
    text(1, 2.2, 'subplot({},{},{})'.format(nrows, ncols, i+1),
        fontsize=14, color='Brown')
```

After defining the figure size in the usual way, we set the number of rows and columns of the grid of axes we want to generate. Then, each of the Axes objects is created and configured in the loop. Look carefully at how the positions of the axes are identified. Note also that we show how to set the background color of the axes.

Animations

We will finish the chapter with a more complex example that illustrates the power that matplotlib gives us. We will create an animation of a forced pendulum, a well-known and much studied example of a dynamic system exhibiting deterministic chaos.

Since this section involves more sophisticated code, we will refrain from using `pylab` and adopt the generally recommended way of importing modules. This makes the code easier to export to a script if we so wish. We also give samples of some of the object-oriented features of matplotlib.

The process of animating a pendulum (or any physical process) is actually very simple: we compute the position of the pendulum at a finite number of times and display the corresponding images in quick succession. So, the code will naturally break down into the following three pieces:

- A function that displays a pendulum in an arbitrary position
- Setting up the computation of the position of the pendulum at an arbitrary time
- The code that actually computes the position of the pendulum and displays the corresponding images

We start by importing all the modules and functions we need to set up the animation:

```
%matplotlib inline
import matplotlib.pyplot as plt
import numpy as np
import matplotlib.patches as patches
import matplotlib.lines as lines
from scipy.integrate import ode
from IPython.display import display, clear_output
import time
```

In the following code, we will define a function that draws a simple sketch of a pendulum:

```
def draw_pendulum(ax, theta, length=5, radius=1):
    v = length * np.array([np.sin(theta), -np.cos(theta)])
    ax.axhline(0.0, color='Brown', lw=5, zorder=0)
    rod = lines.Line2D([0.0, v[0]], [0.0, v[1]],
                        lw=4, color='DarkGray', zorder=1)
    bob = patches.Circle(v, radius,
                        fc='DodgerBlue', ec='DarkSlateGray',
                        lw=1.5, zorder=3)
    peg = patches.Circle([0.0, 0.0], 0.3,
                        fc='black', zorder=2)
    ax.add_patch(bob)
    ax.add_patch(peg)
    ax.add_line(rod)
    return ax
```

This function takes as the first argument an `Axes` object. The other arguments are as follows:

- The angle, `theta`, of the pendulum with the vertical surface
- The `length` of the rod
- The `radius` of the bob

The preceding quantities are indicated in the following figure:

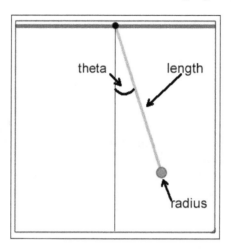

Then, we define a `NumPy` vector, `v`, which holds the position of the pendulum relative to the origin. The following statements define the objects to be drawn:

- `ax.axhline()`: This function draws a horizontal line across the plot
- `rod`: This is a `lines.Line2D` object (incidentally, this is the object that is used to draw most plots in matplotlib)
- `bob` and `peg`: These are objects of the `patches.Circle` type; matplotlib patches represent essentially any kind of object that can be placed in a figure

The following lines of code can be used to test the drawing code:

```
fig = plt.figure(figsize=(5,5))
ax = fig.add_subplot(1, 1, 1)
ax.set_aspect('equal')
ax.set_xlim(-10,10)
ax.set_ylim(-20,0.5)
draw_pendulum(ax, np.pi / 10, length=15, radius=0.5)
ax.set_xticks([])
ax.set_yticks([])
```

Running the code in the previous cell will produce the following image:

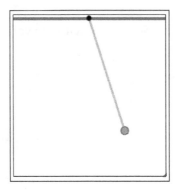

The following comments indicate how the code in the preceding example works:

1. The first two lines define the variables, `fig` and `ax`, that hold the `Figure` and `Axes` objects, respectively. In matplotlib, a `Figure` object is a container that holds all other plotting objects. Each `Figure` can contain several `Axes`, which contain individual plots. Note the use of the `figsize=(5,5)` argument to set the size of the figure.

2. Next, we set the axis limits. The `set_aspect()` method of the ax object is used to set the aspect ratio to be the same in both directions. Without this, the circles will be drawn as ellipses. Then, the `set_xlim()` and `set_ylim()` methods specify the bounds for the axes.

3. We then call the `draw_pendulum()` function, which does all the drawing.

4. Finally, we use `ax.set_xticks([])` and `set_yticks([])` to remove the tick marks from the axes.

The next step is to set up what is needed to find the trajectory to the pendulum. The dynamics of a pendulum are given by a system of differential equations, which is defined in the following lines of code:

```
def pendulum_eq(t, x, c=1, f=lambda t:0.0):
    theta, omega = x
    return np.array([omega,
                    -np.sin(theta) - c * omega + f(t)],
                    dtype=np.float64)
solver = ode(pendulum_eq)
solver.set_integrator('lsoda')
c = 0.3
f = lambda t: 2.0 * np.sin(3 * t)
solver.set_f_params(c, f)
```

This code starts by defining the `pendulum_eq()` function, which stipulates the differential equations for a pendulum. The derivation of the equations is beyond the scope of this book. The remaining code in the cell configures an object of the `ode()` type, which is a part of the `scipy.integrate` module. We will not discuss the details here, but this module is discussed in *Chapter 5, Advanced Computing with SciPy, Numba, and NumbaPro.*

We are now ready to run the animation by executing the following code in a cell:

```
tmax = 20.0
dt = 0.2

fig = plt.figure(1,figsize=(5,5))
ax = plt.subplot(1,1,1)
ax.set_aspect('equal')
ax.set_xlim(-10,10)
ax.set_ylim(-20,0.5)
xtext = -9
ytext = -2
dytext = -1.0

ic = np.array([0.0, 0.3])
solver.set_initial_value(ic, 0.0)
while True:
    clear_output(wait=True)
    time.sleep(1./20)
    t = solver.t
    if t > tmax:
        break
    theta, omega = solver.integrate(t + dt)
    if not solver.successful():
        print 'Solver interrupted'
        break
    ax.clear()
    ax.set_xticks([])
    ax.set_yticks([])
    ax.text(xtext, ytext, r'$t={:5.2f}$'.format(t))
    ax.text(xtext, ytext + dytext,
            r'$\theta={:5.2f}$'.format(theta))
    ax.text(xtext, ytext + 2 * dytext,
            r'$\dot{{\theta}}={:5.2f}$'.format(omega))
    draw_pendulum(ax, theta=theta, length=15, radius=0.5)
    display(fig)
    plt.close()
```

This is probably the most complex code segment in the book so far, but most of it has already been covered. The variables `tmax` and `dt` hold the maximum time for the animation and the time increment, respectively. We then set the `Figure` and `Axes` objects for the plot.

Then comes a `while` loop, where the animation is actually executed. This is the general skeleton of the loop:

```
while True:
    clear_output(wait=True)
    time.sleep(1./20)
    t = solver.t
    if t > tmax:
        break

    ... Code to determine the position of the pendulum...

    ... Code to draw pendulum ...

    display(fig)
    plt.close()
```

 We will not discuss in detail the code used to solve the differential equation since it will be presented in detail in *Chapter 5, Advanced Computing with SciPy, Numba, and NumbaPro*.

The loop has `True` as the looping condition so this is potentially an infinite loop. However, inside the loop, we check if the current time is larger than the maximum time for the animation, and if that is the case, we break from the loop:

```
t = solver.t
if t > tmax:
    break
```

The first thing we do in the loop is to call the `clear_output()` function. This function, as the name indicates, removes the output of the current cell and is at the heart of doing simple animations in the notebook. The `wait=True` argument tells the function to wait until the next image is fully drawn before clearing the output, which prevents flickering.

The `time.sleep(1./20)` argument pauses the computation for a brief period of time to prevent the animation from running too fast. Then, a new position of the pendulum is computed and plotted. Then, `display(fig)` is called to show the figure. This is needed here because, contrary to the case of static graphs, we don't want the plot to be shown only at the end of the cell.

The final detail is to call `plt.close()` at the end of the loop. This prevents the pendulum image from being drawn one extra time when the loop is exited. Placing this call inside the loop also helps to avoid flicker.

The reader is encouraged to play with the parameters of the animation, specially the time interval, `dt`; the maximum time, `tmax`; and the `time.sleep()` parameter. A bit of trial-and-error is needed to get satisfactory animation.

Summary

In this chapter, we learned how to use matplotlib to produce presentation-quality plots. We covered two-dimensional plots and how to set plot options, and annotate and configure plots. You also learned how to add labels, titles, and legends. We also learned how to draw three-dimensional surface plots and how to create simple animations.

In the next chapter, we will explore how to work with data in the notebook using the pandas library.

Handling Data with pandas

In this chapter, we will introduce **pandas**, a powerful and versatile Python library that provides tools for data handling and analysis. We will consider the two main pandas structures for storing data, the `Series` and `DataFrame` objects, in detail. You will learn how to create these structures and how to access and insert data into them. We also cover the important topic of **slicing**, that is, how to access portions of data using the different indexing methods provided by pandas. Next, we'll discuss the computational and graphics tools offered by pandas, and finish the chapter by demonstrating how to work with a realistic dataset.

pandas is an extensive package for data-oriented manipulation, and it is beyond the scope of this book to realistically cover all aspects of the package. We will cover only some of the most useful data structures and functionalities. In particular, we will not cover the `Panel` data structure and multi-indexes. However, we will provide a solid foundation for readers who wish to expand their knowledge by consulting the official package documentation. Throughout this chapter, we assume the following imports:

```
%pylab inline
from pandas import Series, DataFrame
import pandas as pd
```

The Series class

A `Series` object represents a one-dimensional, indexed series of data. It can be thought of as a dictionary, with one main difference: the indexes in a `Series` class are ordered. The following example constructs a `Series` object and displays it:

```
grades1 = Series([76, 82, 78, 100],
                 index = ['Alex', 'Robert', 'Minnie', 'Alice'],
                 name = 'Assignment 1', dtype=float64)

grades1
```

This produces the following output:

```
Alex        76
Robert      82
Minnie      78
Alice      100
Name: Assignment 1, dtype: float64
```

Notice the format of the constructor call:

```
Series(<data>, index=<indexes>, name=<name>, dtype=<type>)
```

Both `data` and `indexes` are usually lists or `NumPy` arrays, but can be any Python iterable. The lists must have the same length. The `name` variable is a string that describes the data in the series. The `type` variable is a `NumPy` data type. The `indexes` and the `name` variables are optional (if `indexes` are omitted, they are set to integers — starting at 0). The data type is also optional, in which case it is inferred from the data.

A `Series` object supports the standard dictionary interface. As an example, run the following code in a cell:

```
print grades1['Minnie']
grades1['Minnie'] = 80
grades1['Theo'] = 92
grades1
```

The output of the preceding command lines is as follows:

```
78.0
Alex        76
Robert      82
Minnie      80
Alice      100
Theo        92
Name: Assignment 1, dtype: float64
```

Here is another interesting example:

```
for student in grades1.keys():
    print '{} got {} points in {}'.format(student,
        grades1[student], grades1.name)
```

The preceding command lines produce the following output:

```
Alex got 76.0 points in Assignment 1
Robert got 82.0 points in Assignment 1
Minnie got 80.0 points in Assignment 1
Alice got 100.0 points in Assignment 1
Theo got 92.0 points in Assignment 1
```

Note that the order of the output is exactly the same as the order in which each of the elements were inserted in the series. Contrary to a standard Python dictionary, the `Series` object keeps track of the order of the elements. In fact, elements can be accessed through an integer index, as shown in the following example:

```
grades1[2]
```

The preceding command returns the following output:

```
80.0
```

Actually, all of Python's list-access interface is supported. For instance, we can use slices, which return `Series` objects:

```
grades1[1:-1]
```

The preceding command gives the following output:

```
Robert      82
Minnie      80
Alice      100
Name: Assignment 1, dtype: float64
```

The indexing capabilities are even more flexible; this is illustrated in the following example:

```
grades1[['Theo', 'Alice']]
```

The preceding command returns the following output:

```
Theo       92
Alice     100
dtype: float64
```

It is also possible to append new data to the series, by using the following command:

```
grades1a = grades1.append(Series([79, 81], index=['Theo', 'Joe']))
grades1a
```

The output of the preceding command is as follows:

```
Alex          76
Robert        82
Minnie        80
Alice        100
Theo          92
Kate          69
Molly         74
Theo          79
Joe           81
dtype:  float64
```

Note that the series now contains two entries corresponding to the key, Theo. This makes sense, since in real-life data there could be more than one data value associated to the same index. In our example, a student might be able to hand in more than one version of the assignment. What happens when we try to access this data? pandas conveniently returns a Series object so that no data is lost:

```
grades1a['Theo']
```

The output of the preceding command is as follows:

```
Theo      92
Theo      79
dtype:  float64
```

> Note that the append() method does not append the values to the existing Series object. Instead, it creates a new object that consists of the original Series object with the appended elements. This behavior is not the same as what happens when elements are appended to a Python list. Quite a few methods of the Series class display behavior that is different from their corresponding list counterparts. A little experimentation (or reading the documentation) may be required to understand the conventions that pandas uses.

Let's define a new series with the following command lines:

```
grades2 = Series([87, 76, 76, 94, 88],
            index = ['Alex', 'Lucy', 'Robert', 'Minnie', 'Alice'],
            name='Assignment 2',
            dtype=float64)
grades2
```

The preceding command lines give the following output:

```
Alex       87
Lucy       76
Robert     76
Minnie     94
Alice      88
Name: Assignment 2, dtype: float64
```

If we want to compute each student's average in the two assignments, we can use the following command:

```
average = 0.5 * (grades1 + grades2)
average
```

On running the preceding code, we get the following output:

```
Alex       81.5
Alice      94.0
Lucy        NaN
Minnie     87.0
Robert     79.0
Theo        NaN
dtype: float64
```

The value NaN stands for **Not a number**, which is a special floating-point value that is used to indicate the result of an invalid operation, such as zero divided by zero. In pandas, it is used to represent a missing data value. We can locate the missing values in Series using the isnull() method. For example, run the following code in a cell:

```
averages.isnull()
```

Running the preceding command line produces the following output:

```
Alex      False
Alice     False
Lucy       True
Minnie    False
Robert    False
Theo       True
dtype: bool
```

If we decide that the missing data can be safely removed from the series, we can use the `dropna()` method:

```
average.dropna()
```

The preceding command line produces the following output:

```
Alex       81.5
Alice      94.0
Minnie     87.0
Robert     79.0
dtype: float64
```

Notice that this is another case in which the original series is not modified.

The `Series` class provides a series of useful methods for its instances. For example, we can sort both the values and the indexes. To sort the values in-place, we use the `sort()` method:

```
grades1.sort()
grades1
```

This generates the following output:

```
Alex        76
Minnie      80
Robert      82
Theo        92
Alice      100
Name: Assignment 1, dtype: float64
```

To sort the indexes of a series, use the `sort_index()` method. For example, consider the following command:

```
grades1.sort_index()
```

This produces the following output:

```
Alex        76
Minnie      80
Robert      82
Theo        92
Alice      100
Name: Assignment 1, dtype: float64
```

Note that the sorting is *not* in-place this time, a new series object is returned.

For the next examples, we will use data on maximum daily temperatures for the month of June from a weather station nearby the author's location. The following command lines generates the series of temperatures for the days from June 6 to June 15:

```
temps = Series([71,76,69,67,74,80,82,70,66,80],
                index=range(6,16),
                name='Temperatures', dtype=float64)
temps
```

The preceding command produces the following output:

```
6        71
7        76
8        69
9        67
10       74
11       80
12       82
13       70
14       66
15       80
Name: Temperatures, dtype: float64
```

Let's first compute the mean and standard deviation of the temperatures using the following command:

```
print temps.mean(), temps.std()
```

The result of the preceding computation is as follows:

```
73.5 5.77831194112
```

If we want a quick overview of the data in the series, we can use the describe() method:

```
temps.describe()
```

The preceding command produces the following output:

```
count     10.000000
mean      73.500000
std        5.778312
min       66.000000
25%       69.250000
50%       72.500000
75%       79.000000
max       82.000000
Name: Temperatures, dtype: float64
```

Note that the information is returned as a `Series` object, so it can be stored in case it is needed in further computations.

To draw a plot of the series, we use the `plot()` method. If we just need a quick graphical overview of the data, we can just run the following command:

```
temps.plot()
```

However, it's also possible to produce nicely formatted, production-quality plots of the data, since all matplotlib features are supported in pandas. The following code illustrates how some of the graph formatting options discussed in *Chapter 3, Graphics with matplotlib*, are being used:

```
temps.plot(style='-s', lw=2, color='green')
axis((6,15,65, 85))
xlabel('Day')
ylabel('Temperature')
title('Maximum daily temperatures in June')
None # prevent text output
```

The preceding command lines produce the following plot:

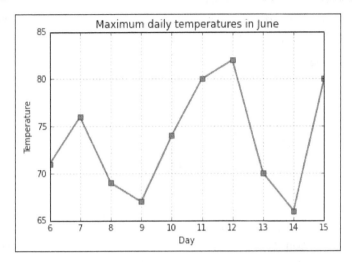

Suppose we want to find the days in which the maximum temperature was above 75 degrees. This can be achieved with the following expression:

```
temps[temps > 75]
```

The preceding command returns the following series:

```
7        76
11       80
12       82
15       80
Name: Temperatures, dtype: float64
```

There are many more useful methods provided by the `Series` class. Remember that in order to see all the available methods, we can use the code completion feature of IPython. Start typing `temps.` and you will get the available methods.

Then press the *Tab* key. A window with a list of all available methods will pop up. You can then explore what is available.

The DataFrame class

The `DataFrame` class is used to represent two-dimensional data. To illustrate its use, let's create a `DataFrame` class containing student data as follows:

```
grades = DataFrame(
    [['Alice',  80., 92., 84,],
     ['Bob',    78., NaN, 86,],
     ['Samaly', 75., 78., 88.]],
    index = [17005, 17035, 17028],
    columns = ['Name', 'Test 1', 'Test 2', 'Final']
    )
```

This code demonstrates one of the most straightforward ways to construct a `DataFrame` class. In the preceding case, the data can be specified as any two-dimensional Python data structure, such as a list of lists (as shown in the example) or a `NumPy` array. The `index` option sets the row names, which are integers representing student IDs here. Likewise, the `columns` option sets the column names. Both the `index` and `column` arguments can be given as any one-dimensional Python structure, such as lists, `NumPy` arrays, or a `Series` object.

To display the output of the `DataFrame` class, run the following statement in a cell:

`grades`

The preceding command displays a nicely formatted table as follows:

	Name	Test 1	Test 2	Final
17005	Alice	80	92	84
17035	Bob	78	NaN	86
17028	Samaly	75	78	88

The `DataFrame` class features an extremely flexible interface for initialization. We suggest that the reader run the following command to know more about it:

`DataFrame?`

This will display information about the construction options. Our goal here is not to cover all possibilities, but to give an idea of the offered flexibility. Run the following code in a cell:

```
idx = pd.Index(["First row", "Second row"])
col1 = Series([1, 2], index=idx)
```

```
col2 = Series([3, 4], index=idx)
data = {"Column 1":col1, "Column2":col2}
df = DataFrame(data)
df
```

The preceding code produces the following table:

	Column 1	Column2
First row	1	3
Second row	2	4

This example illustrates a useful way of thinking of a `DataFrame` object: it consists of a dictionary of `Series` objects with a common `Index` object labeling the rows of the table. Each element in the dictionary corresponds to a column in the table. Keep in mind that this is simply a way to conceptualize a `DataFrame` object, and this is not a description of its internal storage.

Let's go back to our student data example. Let's add a column with the total score of each student, which is the average of the grades, with the final having weight two. This can be computed with the following code:

```
grades.loc[:,'Score'] = 0.25 * (grades['Test 1'] + grades['Test 2'] + 2 *
grades['Final'])
grades
```

The output for the preceding command line is as follows:

	Name	Test 1	Test 2	Final	Score
17005	Alice	80	92	84	85.00
17035	Bob	78	NaN	86	NaN
17028	Samaly	75	78	88	82.25

In the preceding command line, we used one of the following recommended methods of accessing elements from a `DataFrame` class:

- `.loc`: This method is label-based, that is, the element positions are interpreted as labels (of columns or rows) in the table. This method was used in the preceding example.

- `.iloc`: This method is integer-based. The arguments must be integers and are interpreted as zero-based indexes for the rows and columns of the table. For example, `grades.iloc[0,1]` refers to the data in row 0 and column 1, which is Alice's grade in Test 1 in the preceding example.

- `.ix`: This indexing method supports mixed integer and label-based access. For example, both `grades.ix[17035, 4]` and `grades.ix[17035, 'Score']` refer to Bob's score in the course. Notice that pandas is smart enough to know that the row labels are integers, so that the index `17035` refers to a label, not a position in the table. Indeed, attempting to access the `grades.ix[1, 4]` element will flag an error because there is no row with label 1.

To use any of these methods, the corresponding entry (or entries) in the `DataFrame` object must already exist. So, these methods cannot be used to insert or append new data.

Notice that Bob does not have a grade in his second test, indicated by the `NaN` entry (he was probably sick on the day of the test). When he takes a retest, his grade can be updated as follows:

```
grades.loc[17035,'Test 2'] = 98

grades
```

In the output, you will notice that Bob's final score is not automatically updated. This is no surprise because a `DataFrame` object is not designed to work as a spreadsheet program. To perform the update, you must explicitly execute the cell that computes the score again. After you do that, the table will look like this:

	Name	Test 1	Test 2	Final	Score
17005	Alice	80	92	84	85.00
17035	Bob	78	98	86	87.00
17028	Samaly	75	78	88	82.25

It is also possible to use regular indexing to access `DataFrame` entries, but that is frowned upon. For example, to refer to Samaly's grade in the final, we could use the **chained reference**, that is, by using `grades['Test 2'][17028]`. (Notice the order of the indexes!) We will avoid this usage.

The teacher is a little disappointed, because no student got an A grade (score above 90). So, students are given an extra credit assignment. To add a column with the new grade component beside the `Final` column, we can run the following command lines:

```
grades.insert(4, 'Extra credit', [2., 6., 10.])
grades
```

Obviously, we can also insert rows. To add a new student we could use the following command lines:

```
grades.loc[17011,:] = ['George', 92, 88, 91, 9, NaN]
grades
```

Of course, the scores have to be updated as follows to take the extra credit into account:

```
grades.loc[:,'Score'] = 0.25 * (grades['Test 1'] + grades['Test 2'] + 2 *
grades['Final']) + grades['Extra credit']
grades
```

Now, suppose we want to find all students who got an A and had a score of less than 78 in Test 1. We can do this by using a Boolean expression as index, as shown in the following code:

```
grades[(grades['Score'] >= 90) & (grades['Test 1'] < 78)]
```

Two important things should be noted from the preceding example:

- We need to use the `&` operator instead of the `and` operator
- The parentheses are necessary due to the high precedence of the `&` operator

This will return a subtable with the rows that satisfy the condition expressed by the Boolean expression.

Suppose we want the names and scores of the students who have a score of at least 80, but less than 90 (these could represent the "B" students). The following command lines will be useful to do so:

```
grades[(80 <= grades['Score']) & grades['Score'] < 90].loc[:,['Name',
'Score']]]
```

This is what this code does:

- The expression `grades[(80 <= grades['Score']) & grades['Score'] < 90]` creates a `DataFrame` class that contains all student data for students who have a score of at least 80 but less than 90.

- Then, `.loc[:,'Name', 'Score']` takes a slice of this `DataFrame` class, which consists of all rows in the columns labeled `Name` and `Score`.

An important point about pandas data structures is that whenever data is referred to, the returned object may be either a copy or a view of the original data. Let's create a `DataFrame` class with pseudorandom data to see some examples. To make things interesting, each column will contain normal data with a given mean and standard deviation. The code is as follows:

```
means = [0, 0, 1, 1, -1, -1, -2, -2]
sdevs = [1, 2, 1, 2,  1,  2,  1,  2]
random_data = {}
nrows = 30
for mean, sdev in zip(means, sdevs):
    label = 'Mean={}, sd={}'.format(mean, sdev)
    random_data[label] = normal(mean, sdev, nrows)
row_labels = ['Row {}'.format(i) for i in range(nrows)]
dframe = DataFrame(random_data, index=row_labels)
```

The preceding command lines create the data we need for the examples. Perform the following steps:

1. Define the Python lists, `means` and `sdevs`, which contain the mean and standard deviation values of the distributions.

2. Then, create a dictionary named `random_data`, with string keys that correspond to the column labels of the `DataFame` class that will be created.

3. Each entry in the dictionary corresponds to a list of size `nrows` containing the data, which is generated by the function call to the `normal()` function of `NumPy`.

4. Create a list named `row_labels`, which contains row labels of the `DataFrame` class.

5. Use both the data, that is, the `random_data` dictionary and the `row_labels` list, in the `DataFrame` constructor.

The preceding code will generate a table of 30 rows and 8 columns. You can see the table, as usual, by evaluating dframe by itself in a cell. Notice that even though the table is of a moderately large size, the IPython notebook does a good job of displaying it.

Let's now select a slice of the DataFrame class. For the purpose of demonstration, we will use the mixed indexing .ix method:

```
dframe_slice = dframe.ix['Row 3':'Row 11', 5:]
dframe_slice
```

Notice how the ranges are specified:

- The expression 'Row 3':'Row 11' represents a range specified by labels. Notice that, contrary to the usual assumptions in Python, the range includes the last element (Row 11, in this case).
- The expression 5: (the number 5 followed by a colon) represents a range numerically, from the fifth column to the end of the table.

Now, run the following command lines in a cell:

```
dframe_slice.loc['Row 3','Mean=1, sd=2'] = normal(1, 2)
print dframe_slice.loc['Row 3','Mean=1, sd=2']
print dframe.loc['Row 3','Mean=1, sd=2']
```

The first line resamples a single cell in the data table, and the other two rows print the result. Notice that the printed values are the same! This shows that no copying has taken place, and the variable dframe_slice refers to the same objects (memory area) that already existed in the DataFrame class referred to by the dframe variable. (This is the analogous to pointers in languages such as C, where more than one pointer can refer to the same memory. It is, actually, the standard way variables behave in Python: there is no default copying.)

What if we really want a copy? All pandas objects have a copy() method, so we can use the following code:

```
dframe_slice_copy = dframe.ix['Row 3':'Row 11', 5:].copy()
dframe_slice_copy
```

The preceding command lines will produce the same output as the previous example. However, notice what happens if we modify dframe_slice_copy:

```
dframe_slice_copy.loc['Row 3','Mean=1, sd=2'] = normal(1, 2)
print dframe_slice_copy.loc['Row 3','Mean=1, sd=2']
print dframe.loc['Row 3','Mean=1, sd=2']
```

Now the printed values are different, confirming that only the copy was modified.

In certain cases, it is important to know if the data is copied or simply referred to during a slicing operation. Care should be taken, specially, with more complex data structures. Full coverage of this topic is beyond the scope of this book. However, using .loc, .iloc, and .ix as shown in the preceding examples is sufficient to avoid trouble. For an example where *chained indexing* can cause errors, see http://pandas.pydata.org/pandas-docs/stable/indexing.html#indexing-view-versus-copy for more information.

If you ever encounter a warning referring to SettingWithCopy, check if you are trying to modify an entry of a DataFrame object using chained indexing, such as in dframe_object['a_column']['a_row']. Changing the object access to use .loc instead, for example, will eliminate the warning.

To finish this section, let's consider a few more examples of slicing a DataFrame as follows. In all of the following examples, there is no copying; only a new reference to the data is created.

- Slicing with lists as indexes is performed using the following command line:

```
dframe.ix[['Row 12', 'Row 3', 'Row 24'], [3, 7]]
```

- Slicing to reorder columns is performed using the following command line:

```
dframe.iloc[:,[-1::-1]]
```

The preceding example reverses the column order. To have an arbitrary reordering, use a list with a permutation of the column positions:

```
dframe.iloc[:,[2, 7, 0, 1, 3, 4, 6, 5]]
```

Note that there is no actual reordering of columns in the dframe object, since there is no copying of the data.

- Slicing with Boolean operations is performed using the following command line:

```
dframe.loc[dframe.loc[:,'Mean=1, sd=1']>0, 'Mean=1, sd=1']
```

The preceding command line selects the elements in the column labeled Mean=1, sd=1 (that are positive), and returns a Series object (since the data is one-dimensional). If you are having trouble understanding the way this works, run the following command line in a cell by itself:

```
dframe.loc[:,'Mean=1, sd=1']>0
```

This statement will return a `Series` object with Boolean values. The previous command line selects the rows of `dframe` corresponding to the positions that result as `True` in the `Series` object.

- Slicing will, in general, return an object with a different shape than the original. The `where()` method can be used, as follows, in cases where the shape has to be preserved.

```
dframe.where(dframe>0)
```

The preceding command line returns a `DataFrame` class that has missing values (`NaN`) in the entries that correspond to non-negative values of the original `dframe` object.

We can also indicate a value to be replaced by the values that do not satisfy the given condition using the following command line:

```
dframe.where(dframe>0, other=0)
```

This command line will replace the entries corresponding to non-negative values by 0.

Computational and graphics tools

The objects of pandas have a rich set of built-in computational tools. To illustrate some of this functionality, we will use the random data stored in the `dframe` object defined in the previous section. If you discarded that object, here is how to construct it again:

```
means = [0, 0, 1, 1, -1, -1, -2, -2]
sdevs = [1, 2, 1, 2,  1,  2,  1,  2]
random_data = {}
nrows = 30
for mean, sdev in zip(means, sdevs):
    label = 'Mean={}, sd={}'.format(mean, sdev)
    random_data[label] = normal(mean, sdev, nrows)
row_labels = ['Row {}'.format(i) for i in range(nrows)]
dframe = DataFrame(random_data, index=row_labels)
```

Let's explore some of this functionality of the built-in computational tools.

- To get a list of the methods available for the object, start typing the following command in a cell:

```
dframe.
```

- Then, press the *Tab* key. The completion popup allows us to select a method by double clicking on it. For example, double click on `mean`. The cell text changes to the following:

```
dframe.mean
```

- Now, add a question mark to the preceding command line and run the cell:

```
dframe.mean?
```

This will display information about the `mean` method (which, not surprisingly, computes the mean of the data).

Using tab-completion and IPython's help features is an excellent way to learn about pandas' features. I recommend that you always display the documentation this way, at least the first few times a method is used. Learning about the features that pandas offers can be a real time-saver.

Now, let's continue with the functionalities:

- Let's say that we want to compute the column means for our random data. This can be done by evaluating the following command:

```
dframe.mean()
```

- The standard deviation values can be computed with the following command:

```
dframe.std()
```

Note that the results for all of the immediately preceding command lines are returned as `Series` objects, which is the default object type that pandas uses for one-dimensional data. In particular, the column labels become the indexes of the objects. Let's say we want to create a `DataFrame` object containing the mean and standard deviation in two rows. pandas makes this a very easy task, using built-in conversions and constructors.

```
mean_series = dframe.mean()
std_series = dframe.std()
mean_std = DataFrame([dict(mean_series),
                      dict(std_series)],
                     index=['mean', 'std'])

mean_std
```

In this code, we first compute the means and standard deviations and assign them to variables for clarity. Then, we call the `DataFrame` constructor that accepts a list of Python dictionaries. This is made easy because pandas allows conversion from a `Series` object to a dictionary in a convenient way: `dict(mean_series)` returns the representation of `mean_series` as a dictionary, using the indexes of the `Series` object as keys to the dictionary.

Let's say we want to standardize the data in all columns so that they all have a common mean value 100 and standard deviation value 20. This can be achieved using the following command lines:

```
dframe_stnd = 100 + 20 * (dframe - mean_std.iloc[0,:]) / mean_std.iloc[1,:]
dframe_stnd
```

The preceding command lines simply implement the definition of standardization: we subtract the means from the data, divide by the standard deviation, scale by the desired value of the deviation, and add the desired mean. To check that we get the expected results, run the following command lines:

```
print dframe_stnd.mean()
print dframe_stnd.std()
```

To illustrate the possibilities, let's do a two-sided test of the hypothesis that the mean of each column is 0. We first compute the **Z-scores** for the columns. The Z-score of each column is just the deviation from the column mean to the model mean (0 in this case), properly scaled by the standard deviation:

```
zscores = mean_std.iloc[0,:] / (mean_std.iloc[1,:] / sqrt(len(dframe)))
zscores
```

The scaling factor, `sqrt(len(dframe))`, is the square root of the number of data points, which is given by the number of rows in the table. The last step is to compute the **p-values** for each column. The p-values are simply a measure of the probability that the data deviates from the mean by more than the corresponding Z-score, given the assumed distribution. These values are obtained from a normal distribution (technically, we should use a **t-distribution**, since we are using the sample standard deviation, but in this example this does not really make any difference, since the data is normally generated, and the sample size is large enough). The following command lines use the normal distribution object, `norm`, from SciPy to compute the p-values as percentages:

```
from scipy.stats import norm
pvalues = 2 * norm.cdf(-abs(zscores)) * 100
pvalues_series = Series(pvalues, index = zscores.index)
pvalues_series
```

The line that computes the p-values is as follows:

```
pvalues = 2 * norm.cdf(-abs(zscores)) * 100
```

We use the `cdf()` method, which computes the cumulative distribution function for the normal curve from the `norm` object. We then multiply it with 2, since this is a two-sided test, and multiply by 100 to get a percentage.

The next line converts the p-values into a `Series` object. This is not necessary, but makes the results easier to visualize.

The following are the results obtained:

```
Mean=-1, sd=1    1.374183e-02
Mean=-1, sd=2    1.541008e-01
Mean=-2, sd=1    2.812333e-26
Mean=-2, sd=2    1.323917e-04
Mean=0,  sd=1    2.840077e+01
Mean=0,  sd=2    6.402502e+01
Mean=1,  sd=1    2.182986e-06
Mean=1,  sd=2    5.678316e-01
dtype: float64
```

 Please note that in the preceding example, you will get different numbers, since the data is randomly generated.

The results are what we expect, given the way the data was generated: the p-values are all very small, except for the columns that have mean 0.

Now, let's explore some of the graphical capabilities provided by pandas. The pandas plots are produced using matplotlib, so the basic interface has already been discussed in *Chapter 3*, *Graphics with matplotlib*. In the examples that follow, we will assume that we are using the magic. Run the following command in the cell:

```
%pylab inline
```

Most of the plotting capabilities of pandas are implemented as methods of `Series` or `DataFrame` objects.

Let's define the following data in our table to include more data points:

```
means = [0, 0, 1, 1, -1, -1, -2, -2]
```

```
sdevs = [1, 2, 1, 2,  1,  2,  1,  2]
random_data = {}
nrows = 300
for mean, sdev in zip(means, sdevs):
    label = 'Mean={}, sd={}'.format(mean, sdev)
    random_data[label] = normal(mean, sdev, nrows)
row_labels = ['Row {}'.format(i) for i in range(nrows)]
dframe = DataFrame(random_data, index=row_labels)
```

To display a grid of histograms of the data, we can use the following command:

```
dframe.hist(color='DarkCyan')
subplots_adjust(left=0.5, right=2, top=2.5, bottom=1.0)
```

We use the `hist()` method to generate the histograms and use the `color` option as well, which is passed to the matplotlib function calls that actually do the drawing. The second line of code adds spaces to the plots so that the axis labels do not overlap. You may find that some of the histograms do not look normal. To fix their appearance, it is possible to fiddle with the `bins` and `range` options of the `hist()` method, as shown in the following example:

```
dframe.loc[:,'Mean=0, sd=2'].hist(bins=40, range=(-10,10),
color='LightYellow')
title('Normal variates, mean 0, standard deviation 2')
```

This will draw a histogram of the data in the column for a mean of `0` and standard deviation of `2`, with `40` bins in the range from `-10` to `10`. In other words, each bin will have a width of `0.5`. Note that the plot may not include all the range from `-10` to `10`, since pandas restricts the drawing to ranges that actually contain data.

For example, let's generate data according to **Geometrical Brownian Motion (GBM)**, which is a model used in mathematical finance to represent the evolution of stock prices. (For details, see `http://en.wikipedia.org/wiki/Geometric_Brownian_motion`.) This model is defined in terms of two parameters, representing the **percentage drift** and **percentage volatility** of the stock. We start by defining these two values in our model, as well as the initial value of the stock:

```
mu = 0.15
sigma = 0.33
S0 = 150
```

The simulation should run from time `0.0` to the maximum time `20.0`, and we want to generate 200 data points. The following command lines define these parameters:

```
nsteps = 200
tmax = 20.
dt = tmax/nsteps
times = arange(0, tmax, dt)
```

The stock model would naturally be represented by a time series (a `Series` object). However, to make the simulation simpler, we will use a `DataFame` object and build the simulation column by column. We will start with a very simple table containing only integer indexes and the simulation times:

```
gbm_data = DataFrame(times, columns=['t'], index=range(nsteps))
```

To see the first few rows of the table, we can use the following command line:

```
gbm_data.loc[:5,:]
```

You might want to run this command after each column is added in order to get a better idea of how the simulation progresses.

The basis for the GBM model is (unsurprisingly) a stochastic process called **Brownian Motion (BM)**. This process has two parts. A deterministic component, called **drift**, is computed as follows:

```
gbm_data['drift'] = (mu - sigma**2/2) * gbm_data.loc[:,'t']
```

The next component adds randomness. It is defined in terms of increments, which are normally distributed with mean zero and standard deviation given by the time interval multiplied by the percentage volatility:

```
gbm_data['dW'] = normal(0.0, sigma * dt, nsteps)
```

The BM component is then defined as the cumulative sum of the increments, as shown in the following command lines:

```
gbm_data['W'] = gbm_data.loc[:,'dW'].cumsum()
gbm_data.ix[0, 'W'] = 0.0
```

In the preceding command lines, we add the second line because we want the process to start at `0`, which is not the convention adopted by the `cumsum()` method.

We are now ready to compute the stock simulation. It is calculated by taking the drift component, adding to the BM component, taking the exponential of the result, and finally, multiplying it by the initial value of the stock. This is all done with the following command:

```
gbm_data['S'] = S0 * exp(gbm_data.loc[:,'drift'] + gbm_data.loc[:,'W'])
```

We are now ready to plot the result of the simulation using the following command lines:

```
gbm_data.plot(x='t', y='S', lw=2, color='green',
              title='Geometric Brownian Motion')
```

The preceding command lines produce the following graph. Obviously, the graph you will get will be different due to randomness.

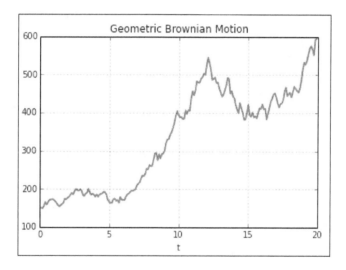

An example with a realistic dataset

In this section, we will work with a realistic dataset of moderate size. We will use the **World Development Indicators** dataset, which is provided free of charge by the World Bank. This is a reasonably sized dataset that is not too large or complex to experiment with.

In any real application, we will need to read data from some source, reformat it to our purposes, and save the reformatted data back to some storage system. pandas offers facilities for data retrieval and storage in multiple formats:

- **Comma-separated values (CSV)** in text files
- Excel
- JSON
- SQL
- HTML
- Stata
- Clipboard data in text format
- Python-pickled data

The list of formats supported by pandas keeps growing with each new update to the library. Please refer to `http://pandas.pydata.org/pandas-docs/stable/io.html` for a current list.

Treating all formats supported by pandas is not possible in a book with the current scope. We will restrict examples to CSV files, which is a simple text format that is widely used. Most software packages and data sources have options to format data as CSV files.

Curiously enough, CSV is not a formally described storage format. pandas does a good job of providing enough options to read the great majority of files. However, the format of the data may vary depending on the data source. Luckily, since CSV files are simply text files, we can open the files in a spreadsheet program or even a text editor to examine their structure.

The dataset for this section can be downloaded from `http://data.worldbank.org/data-catalog/world-development-indicators`, and is also available in the book website. If you choose to download the data from the original website, make sure you choose the CSV file format. The file is in compressed ZIP format, and is about 40 MB in size. Once the archive is decompressed, we get the following files.

- `WDI_Country.csv`
- `WDI_CS_Notes.csv`
- `WDI_Data.csv`
- `WDI_Description.csv`
- `WDI_Footnotes.csv`
- `WDI_Series.csv`
- `WDI_ST_Notes.csv`

As is typical of any realistic dataset, there's always a lot of ancillary information associated with the data. This is called **metadata** and is used to give information about the dataset, including things such as the labels used for rows and/or columns, data collection details, and explanations concerning the meaning of the data. The metadata is contained in the various files contained within the archive. The reader is encouraged to open the different files using spreadsheet software (or a text editor) to get a feel for the kind of information available. For us, the most important metadata file is `WDI_Series.csv`, which contains information on the meaning of data labels for the several time series contained in the data.

The actual data is in the `WDI_Data.csv` file. As this file contains some of the metadata information, we will be able to do all the work using this file only.

Make sure the `WDI_Data.csv` file is in the same directory that contains your IPython notebook files, and run the following command in a cell:

```
wdi = pd.read_csv('WDI_Data.csv')
```

This will read the file and store it in a `DataFrame` object that we assign to the variable, `wdi`. The first row in the file is assumed to contain the column labels by default. We can see the beginning of the table by running the following command:

```
wdi.loc[:5]
```

Note that the `DataFrame` class is indexed by integers by default. It is possible to choose one of the columns in the data file as the index by passing the `index_col` parameter to the `read_csv()` method. The index column can be specified either by its position or by its label in the file. The many options available to `read_csv()` are discussed in detail at `http://pandas.pydata.org/pandas-docs/stable/io.html#io-read-csv-table`.

An examination of the file shows that it will need some work to be put in a format that can be easily used. Each row of the file contains a time series of annual data corresponding to one country and economic indicator. One initial step is to get all the countries and economic indicators contained in the file. To get a list of unique country names, we can use the following command line:

```
countries = wdi.loc[:, 'Country Name'].unique()
```

To see how many countries are represented, run the following command line:

```
len(countries)
```

Some of the entries in the file actually correspond to groups of countries, such as Sub-Saharan Africa.

Now, for indicators, we can run the following command line:

```
indicators = wdi.loc[:,'Indicator Code'].unique()
```

There are more than 1300 different economic indicators in the file. This can be verified by running the following command line:

```
len(indicators)
```

To show the different kinds of computation one might be interested in performing, let's consider a single country, for example, Brazil. Let's also suppose that we are only interested on the **Gross Domestic Product (GDP)** information. Now, we'll see how to select the data we are interested in from the table. To make the example simpler, we will perform the selection in two steps. First, we select all rows for the country name Brazil, using the following command line:

```
wdi_br = wdi.loc[wdi.loc[:,'Country Name']=='Brazil',:]
```

In the code preceding command line, consider the following expression:

```
wdi.loc[:,'Country Name']=='Brazil'
```

This selects all the rows in which the country name string is equal to Brazil. For these rows, we want to select all columns of the table, as indicated by the colon in the first term of the slicing operation.

Let's now select all the rows that refer to the GDP data. We start by defining a function that, given a string, determines if it contains the substring GDP (ignoring the case):

```
select_fcn = lambda string: string.upper().find('GDP') >= 0
```

We now want to select the rows in wdi_br that return True when select_fcn is applied to the Indicator Code column. This can be done with the following command lines:

```
criterion = wdi_br.loc[:,'Indicator Code'].map(select_fcn)
wdi_br_gdp = wdi_br.loc[criterion,:]
```

The map() method of the Series object does exactly what we want: it applies a function to all elements of a series. We assign the result of this call to the variable, criterion. Then, we use criterion in the slicing operation that defines wdi_br_gdp. To see how many rows were selected, run the following command:

```
len(wdi_br_gdp)
```

In the dataset used at the writing of this book, the preceding command returns `32`. This means that there are 32 GDP-related indicators for the country named `Brazil`. Since we now have a manageable amount of data, we can display a table that has the indicator codes and their meanings using the following command line:

```
wdi_br_gdp.loc[:,['Indicator Code', 'Indicator Name']]
```

The preceding command line generates a nicely formatted table of the indicator and corresponding names, as shown in the following table:

	Indicator Code	Indicator Name
37625	NY.GDP.COAL.RT.ZS	Coal rents (% of GDP)
37722	NY.GDP.DISC.KN	Discrepancy in expenditure estimate of GDP (co…
37723	NY.GDP.DISC.CN	Discrepancy in expenditure estimate of GDP (cu…
37851	NY.GDP.FRST.RT.ZS	Forest rents (% of GDP)
37855	NY.GDP.MKTP.KD	GDP (constant 2005 US$)
37856	NY.GDP.MKTP.KN	GDP (constant LCU)
37857	NY.GDP.MKTP.CN	GDP (current LCU)
37858	NY.GDP.MKTP.CD	GDP (current US$)
37859	NY.GDP.DEFL.ZS	GDP deflator (base year varies by country)
37860	NY.GDP.MKTP.KD.ZG	GDP growth (annual %)
37861	NY.GDP.PCAP.KD	GDP per capita (constant 2005 US$)

Let's say that we are interested only in four indicators: the GDP, annual GDP growth, GDP per capita, and GDP per capita growth. We can further trim the data with the following command:

```
wdi_br_gdp = wdi_br_gdp.loc[[37858, 37860, 37864, 37865], :]
```

This produces quite a manageable table with 4 rows and 58 columns. Each row contains a time series of the corresponding GDP data starting with the year 1960.

The problem with this table as it is laid out is that it is the "transpose" of what is the usual convention in pandas: the time series are across the rows of the table, instead of being down the columns. So, we still need to do a little more work with our table. We want the indexes of our table to be the years. We also want to have one column for each economic indicator and want to use the economic indicator names (not the codes) as the labels of the columns. Here is how this can be done:

```
idx = wdi_br_gdp.loc[:,'1960':].columns
cols = wdi_br_gdp.loc[:,'Indicator Name']
data = wdi_br_gdp.loc[:,'1960':].as_matrix()
br_data = DataFrame(data.transpose(), columns=cols, index=idx)
```

The following is an explanation of what the preceding command lines do:

1. We first define an `Index` object corresponding to the years in the table using the `columns` field of the `DataFrame` object. The object is stored in the variable `idx`.

2. Then, we create an object containing the column names. This is a `Series` object stored in the variable `cols`.

3. Next, we extract the data we are interested in, that is, the portion of the table corresponding to the years after 1960. We use the `as_matrix()` method of the `DataFrame` object to convert the data to a `NumPy` array, and store it in the variable `data`.

4. Finally, we call the `DataFrame` constructor to create the new table.

Now that we have the data we want in a nice format, it is a good time to save it:

```
br_data.to_csv('WDI_Brazil_GDP.csv')
```

At this point, we can open the `WDI_Brazil_GDP.csv` file in a spreadsheet program to view it.

Now, let's start playing with the data by creating a few plots. Let's first plot the GDP and GDP growth, starting in 1980. Since the data is given in dollars, we scale to give values in billions of dollars.

```
pdata = br_data.ix['1970':, 0] / 1E9
pdata.plot(color='DarkRed', lw=2,
            title='Brazil GDP, billions of current US$')
```

The preceding command lines produce the following chart:

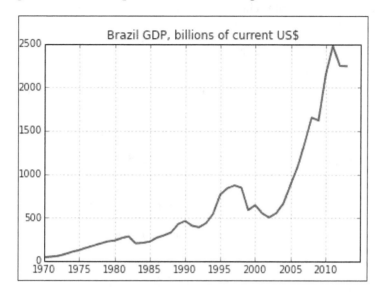

As a final example, let's draw a chart comparing the percent growth of per capita GDP for the **BRIC (Brazil, Russia, India, and China)** countries in the period 2000 to 2010. Since we already have explored the structure of the data, the task is somewhat simpler:

```
bric_countries = ['Brazil', 'China', 'India', 'Russian Federation']
gdp_code = 'NY.GDP.PCAP.KD.ZG'
selection_fct = lambda s: s in bric_countries
criterion = wdi.loc[:,'Country Name'].map(selection_fct)
wdi_bric = wdi.loc[criterion & (wdi.loc[:,'Indicator Code'] == gdp_code),:]
```

We first define a list with the names of the BRIC countries and a string with the indicator code for percent GDP growth per capita. Then, we define a selection function: a string is selected if it is one of the BRIC country names. The map() method is then used to apply the selection function to all entries of the Country Name column. The last command line performs the actual selection. Note the use of the Boolean operator & to combine the two criteria used in the row selection.

We now perform the reformatting of the data to have the relevant data series along the columns of the table. The command lines are similar to the ones in the previous example:

```
df_temp = wdi_bric.loc[:, '2000':'2010']
idx = df_temp.columns
cols = wdi_bric.loc[:, 'Country Name']
data = df_temp.as_matrix()
bric_gdp = DataFrame(data.transpose(), columns=cols, index=idx)
```

Once this is done, plotting the data is straightforward:

```
bric_gdp.plot(lw=2.5,
              title='Annual per capita GDP growth (%)')
```

The preceding command lines result in the following plot:

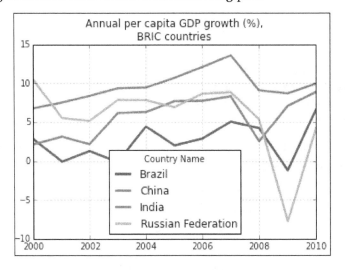

Summary

In this chapter, we covered the objects of pandas, `Series` and `DataFrame`, which are specialized containers for data-oriented computations. We discussed how to create, access, and modify these objects, including advanced indexing and slicing operations. We also considered the computational and graphical capabilities offered by pandas. We then discussed how these capabilities can be leveraged to work with a realistic dataset.

In the next chapter, we will learn how to use SciPy to solve advanced mathematical problems of modeling, science, and engineering.

5
Advanced Computing with SciPy, Numba, and NumbaPro

In this chapter, the user will learn how to use `SciPy` to perform scientific computations. The `Numba` package will then be introduced as a way to accelerate computations. Finally, the `NumbaPro` capabilities of parallel execution in the GPU will be presented.

In this chapter, we will cover the following topics:

- Overview of `SciPy`
- Advanced mathematical algorithms with `SciPy`
- Accelerating computations with `Numba` and `NumbaPro`

Before running the examples in this chapter, load `pylab` by running the following command in a computing cell:

```
%pylab inline
```

Overview of SciPy

`SciPy` is an extensive library for applied mathematics and scientific computation. The following is the complete list of all the modules available in the library:

Module	Functionality
cluster	Clustering algorithms
constants	Physical and mathematical constants
fftpack	Fast Fourier Transform

Module	Functionality
`integrate`	Integration and ordinary differential equations
`interpolate`	Interpolation and splines
`io`	Input and output
`linalg`	Linear algebra
`ndimage`	Image processing
`odr`	Orthogonal distance regression
`optimize`	Optimization and root-finding
`signal`	Signal processing
`sparse`	Sparse matrices
`spatial`	Spatial data structures
`special`	Special functions
`stats`	Statistical distributions
`weave`	C/C++ integration

The standard way to import `SciPy` modules in scripts is using the following command line:

```
from scipy import signal
```

Then, individual functions can be called with the usual module reference syntax, as follows:

```
signal.correlate(…)
```

However, many of the most used functions are available at the top level of the `SciPy` hierarchy. Also, we use IPython in the interactive mode and use (as we assume in this book) the magic, as follows:

```
%pylab inline
```

Many of the functions will be available without explicit module reference.

In the next section, we present a sample of the functions available in `SciPy`. The reader is not expected to know the mathematical techniques and algorithms that will be used in the examples in depth.

Advanced mathematical algorithms with SciPy

In this section, we will cover some of the algorithms available in `SciPy`. Each of the following subsections features a representative example from a significant area of applied science. The examples are chosen so as not to require extensive domain knowledge but still be realistic. These are the topics and examples that we present:

- **Solving equations and finding optimal values**: We will study a market model that requires the solution of a nonlinear system and a facility location problem requiring a nonstandard optimization.

- **Calculus and differential equations**: We will present a volume calculation that uses integral calculus, and **Newton's canon**, a thought experiment proposed by Isaac Newton, which we will model using a system of differential equations. Finally, we will present a three-dimensional system, the famous Lorenz equations, which is an early example displaying chaotic behavior.

Solving equations and finding optimal values

To illustrate this topic, we use a standard supply-versus-demand model from economics. In this model, supply and demand are related to prices by functional relationships, and the equilibrium market is found by determining the intersection of the supply and demand curves. The mathematical formulae we use in the example are somewhat arbitrary (thus possibly unrealistic) but will go beyond what is found in textbooks, where supply and demand are in general assumed to be linear.

The formulae that specify the supply and demand curves are as follows:

$$\text{supply}(q) = \frac{K}{1 + L * q}$$
$$\text{demand(q)} = \frac{Aq}{C - Bq}$$

We will use the *function factory* pattern. Run the following lines of code in a cell:

```
def make_supply(A, B, C):
    def supply_func(q):
        return A * q / (C  - B * q)
    return supply_func
def make_demand(K, L):
    def demand_func(q):
```

```
        return K / (1 + L * q)
    return demand_func
```

The preceding code doesn't directly define the supply and demand curves. Instead, it specifies function factories. This approach makes it easier to work with parameters, which is what we normally want to do in applied problems since we expect the same model to be applicable to a variety of situations.

Next, we set the parameter values and call the function factories to define the functions that actually evaluate the supply and demand curves, as follows:

```
A, B, C = 23.3, 9.2, 82.4
K, L = 1.2, 0.54
supply = make_supply(A, B, C)
demand = make_demand(K, L)
```

The following lines of code make a graph of the curves:

```
q = linspace(0.01,5,200)
plot(q, supply(q), lw = 2)
plot(q, demand(q), lw = 2)
title('Supply and demand curves')
xlabel('Quantity (thousands of units)')
ylabel('Price ($)')
legend(['Supply', 'Demand'], loc='upper left')
```

The following is the graph that is the output of the preceding lines of code:

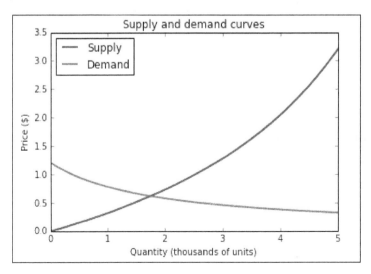

The curves chosen for supply and demand reflect what would be reasonable assumptions: supply increases and demand decreases as the price gets higher. Even with a zero price, the demand is finite (reflecting the fact that there is a limited population interested in the product). On the other hand, the supply curve has a vertical asymptote (not shown in the plot), indicating that there is a production limit (so, even if the price goes to infinity, there is a limited quantity that can be offered in the market).

The equilibrium point of the market is the intersection of the supply and demand curves. To find the equilibrium, we use the `optimize` module, which, besides providing functions for optimization, also has functions to solve numerical equations. The recommended function to find solutions for one-variable functions is `brentq()`, as illustrated in the following code:

```
from scipy import optimize
def opt_func(q):
    return supply(q) - demand(q)
q_eq = optimize.brentq(opt_func, 1.0, 2.0)
print q_eq, supply(q_eq), demand(q_eq)
```

The `brentq()` function assumes that the right-hand side of the equation we want to solve is `0`. So, we start by defining the `opt_func()` function that computes the difference between supply and demand. This function is the first argument of `brentq()`. The next two numerical arguments give an interval that contains the solutions. It is important to choose an interval that contains exactly one solution of the equation. In our example, this is easily done by looking at the graph, from which it is clear that the curves intersect between 1 and 2.

Running the preceding code produces the following output:

```
1.75322153719 0.616415252177 0.616415252177
```

The first value is the equilibrium point, which is the number of units (in thousands) that can be sold at the optimal price. The optimal price is computed using both the supply and demand curves (to check that the values are indeed the same).

To illustrate an optimization problem in two variables, let's consider a problem of optimal facility location. Suppose a factory has several manufacturing stations that need materials to be distributed from a single supply station. The factory floor is rectangular, and the distribution rails must be parallel to the walls of the factory. This last requirement is what makes the problem interesting. The function to be minimized is related to the so-called **taxicab distance**, which is illustrated in the following image:

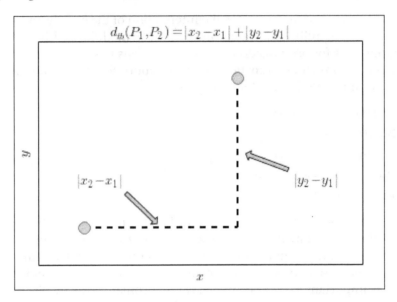

The first step is to define the points where the manufacturing stations are given, as follows:

```
points = array([[10.3,15.4],[6.5,8.8],[15.6,10.3],[4.7,12.8]])
```

The positions are stored as a 4 x 2 NumPy array called `points`, with one point in each row. The following command produces a plot of the points mentioned in the previous command line:

```
plot(points[:,0],points[:,1], 'o', ms=12, mfc='LightSkyBlue')
```

The points are displayed using a circular marker specified by the argument o, which also turns off the line segments connecting the points. The ms and mfc options specify the size of the marker (in pixels) and its color, respectively. The following image is then generated as the output:

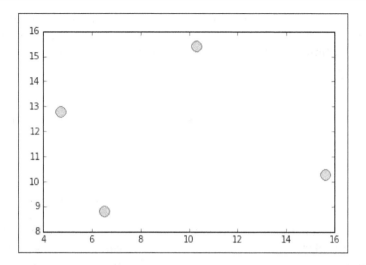

The next step is to define the function to be minimized. We again prefer the approach of defining a function factory, as follows:

```
def make_txmin(points):
    def txmin_func(p):
        return sum(abs(points - p))
    return txmin_func
```

The main point of this code is the way in which the taxicab distance is computed, which takes full advantage of the flexibility of the array operations of NumPy. This is done in the following line of code:

```
return sum(abs(points - p))
```

This code first computes the vector difference, points-p. Note that, here, points is a 4 x 2 array, while p is a 1 x 2 array. NumPy realizes that the dimensions of the arrays are different and uses its *broadcasting rules*. The effect is that the array p is subtracted from each row of the points array, which is exactly what we want. Then the abs() function computes the absolute value of each of the entries of the resulting array, and finally sum() adds all the entries. That's a lot of work done in a single line of code!

We then have to use the function factory to define the function that will actually compute the taxicab distance.

```
txmin = make_txmin(points)
```

The function factory is simply called with the array containing the actual positions as its argument. At this point, the problem is completely set up, and we are ready to compute the optimum, which is done with the following code:

```
from scipy import optimize
x0 = array([0.,0.])
res = optimize.minimize(
        txmin, x0,
        method='nelder-mead',
        options={'xtol':1e-5, 'disp':True})
```

The minimization is computed by a call to the `minimize()` function. The first two arguments of this function are the objective function defined in the previous cell, `txmin()`, and an initial guess, `x0`. We just choose the origin as the initial guess, but in a real-world problem, we use any information we can gather to select a guess that is close to the actual minimum. Several optimization methods are available, suitable for different types of objective functions. We use the **Nelder-Mead method**, which is a heuristic algorithm that does not require smoothness of the objective function. This is well suited for the problem at hand. Finally, we specify two options for the method: the desired tolerance and a display option to print diagnostics. This produces the following output:

```
Optimization terminated successfully.
        Current function value: 23.800000
        Iterations: 87
        Function evaluations: 194
```

The preceding output states that a minimum was successfully found and gives its value. Note that, as in any numerical optimization method, in general, it can only be guaranteed that a local minimum was found. In this case, since the objective function is convex, the minimum is guaranteed to be global. The result of the function is stored in a `SciPy` data structure of the `OptimizeResult` type defined in the `optimize` module. To get the optimal position of the facility, we can use the following command:

```
print res.x
```

The output of the preceding command is as follows:

```
[  8.37782286  11.36247412]
```

To finish this example, we present the code that displays the optimal solution:

```
plot(points[:,0],points[:,1], 'o', ms=12, mfc='LightSkyBlue')
plot(res.x[0], res.x[1],'o', ms=12, mfc='LightYellow')
```

```
locstr = 'x={:5.2f}, y={:5.2f}'.format(res.x[0], res.x[1])
title('Optimal facility location: {}'.format(locstr))
```

The calls to the `plot()` function are similar to the ones in the previous example. To give a nicely formatted title, we first define the `locstr` string, which displays the optimal location coordinates. This is a Python-formatted string with the format specification of `{:5.2f}`, that is, a floating-point field with width 5 and a precision of 2 digits. The result is the following figure:

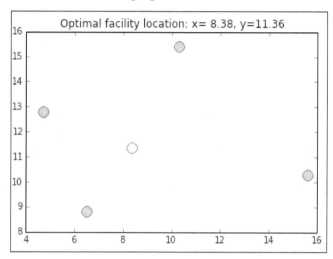

Calculus and differential equations

As an example of a calculus computation, we will show you how to compute the volume of a solid of revolution. The solid is created by rotating the curve displayed in the following figure around the *y*-axis:

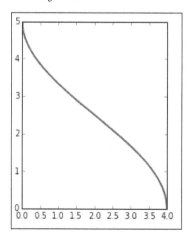

This curve is plotted with the following code:

```
def make_gen(a,b):
    def gen_func(y):
        return a/pi * arccos(2.0 * y / b - 1.0)
    return gen_func
a = 5.
b = 4.
gen = make_gen(a,b)
x = linspace(0,b,200)
y = gen(x)
subplot(111, aspect='equal')
plot(x,y,lw=2)
```

The curve is essentially a stretched and transposed inverse cosine function, as defined in the make_gen() function. It depends on two parameters, a and b, that specify its height and length, respectively. The make_gen() function is a function factory that returns a function that actually computes values in the curve. The actual function defining the curve is called gen() (for *generator*), so this is the function that is plotted.

When this curve is rotated around the vertical axis, we obtain the solid plotted as follows:

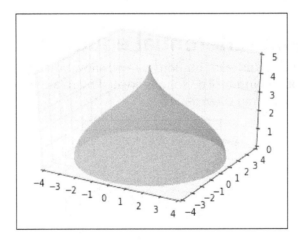

The preceding figure, of course, was generated with IPython using the following code:

```
from mpl_toolkits.mplot3d import Axes3D
na = 50
```

```
nr = 50
avalues = linspace(0, 2*pi, na, endpoint=False)
rvalues = linspace(b/nr, b, nr)
avalues_r = repeat(avalues[...,newaxis], nr, axis=1)
xvalues = append(0, (rvalues*cos(avalues_r)).flatten())
yvalues = append(0, (rvalues*sin(avalues_r)).flatten())
zvalues = gen(sqrt(xvalues*xvalues+yvalues*yvalues))
fig = plt.figure()
ax = fig.gca(projection='3d')
ax.plot_trisurf(xvalues, yvalues, zvalues,
            color='Cyan',alpha=0.65,linewidth=0.)
```

The key function in this code is the call to `plot_trisurf()` in the last line. This function accepts three NumPy arrays, `xvalues`, `yvalues`, and `zvalues`, specifying the coordinates of the points on the surface. The arrays, `xvalues` and `yvalues` define points in a succession of concentric circles, as shown in the following image:

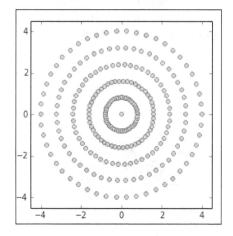

The value of the z coordinate is obtained by computing `gen(sqrt(x*x+y*y))` at each of these points, which has the effect of assigning the same height in the 3D plot to all points of each concentric circle.

To compute the volume of the solid, we use the method of cylindrical shells. An explanation of how the method works is beyond the scope of this book, but it boils down to computing an integral, as shown in the following formula:

$$\int_{x_1}^{x_2} 2\pi x f(x)\, dx$$

In this formula, the *f(x)* function represents the curve being rotated around the y-axis. To compute this integral, we use the `scipy.integrate` package. We use the `quad()` function, which is appropriate for the generic integration of functions that do not have singularities. The following is the code for this formula:

```
import scipy.integrate as integrate

int_func  = lambda x: 2 * pi * x * gen(x)

integrate.quad(int_func, 0, b)
```

After importing the `integrate` module, we define the function to be integrated. Note that we use the `lambda` syntax since this is a one-line calculation. Finally, we call `quad()` to perform the integration. The arguments to the call are the function being integrated and the bounds of integration (from `0` to `b` in this case). The following is the output of the preceding lines of code:

```
(94.24777961000055, 1.440860870616234e-07)
```

The first number is the value of the integral, and the second one is an error estimate.

In the next example, we consider *Newton's canon*, a thought experiment at the very root of modern physics and calculus. The situation is illustrated in the following image, which is an engraving from the book by Sir Isaac Newton, *A Treatise of The System of the World*:

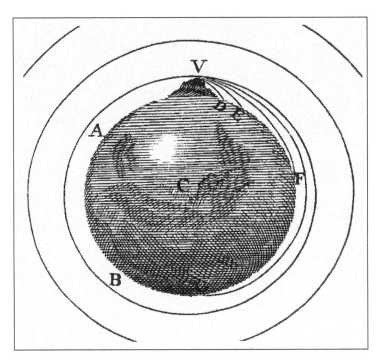

Newton asks us to imagine a canon sitting at the top of a very high mountain. If the canon shoots a projectile, it will fly for a while and eventually hit the ground. The larger the initial velocity of the projectile, the further away it will hit the ground. Let's imagine that we can shoot the projectile as fast as we want, and that there is no air resistance. Then, as the initial velocity increases, eventually the projectile will go around the earth and, if the canon is removed quickly enough, then the projectile will continue its orbit around Earth forever. Newton used this example to explain how the moon could revolve around Earth without ever falling under the action of gravity alone.

To model this situation, we need to use Newton's law of gravitation as a system of differential equations:

$$\frac{dx_1}{dt} = v_1$$

$$\frac{dx_2}{dt} = v_2$$

$$\frac{dv_1}{dt} = -GM \frac{x_1}{(x_1^2 + x_2^2)^{3/2}}$$

$$\frac{dv_2}{dt} = -GM \frac{x_2}{(x_1^2 + x_2^2)^{3/2}}$$

We will not attempt to explain how these formulae were obtained, with the only important point for us being that there are four state variables, with the first two representing the position of the projectile and the last two representing its velocity vector. Since the movement takes place in a plane through the center of Earth, only two position variables are needed. G and M are constants representing Newton's universal gravitational constant and the mass of Earth, respectively. The mass of the projectile does not appear, since the gravitational mass is exactly cancelled by the inertial mass.

The first step to solve this using `SciPy` is to define this set of differential equations, which is done with the following code:

```
M = 5.9726E24
G = 6.67384E-11
C = G * M
def ode_func(xvec, t):
```

```
x1, x2, v1, v2 = xvec
d = (x1 * x1 + x2 * x2) ** 1.5
return array([v1, v2, -C * x1 / d, -C * x2 / d ])
```

All that we need to do is define a function that computes the right-hand side of the system of differential equations. We start by defining the constants, M and G (using SI units), and the auxiliary constant C, since G and M only appear in the equations through their product. The system is represented by the ode_func() function. This function must accept at least two parameters: a NumPy array, xvec, and a floating-point value, t. In our case, xvec is a four-dimensional vector since there are four state variables in our system. The variable, t, is not used in the system since there are no external forces (as there would be if we were launching a rocket instead of shooting a projectile). However, it must still be listed as an input parameter.

Inside ode_func(), we first extract the elements of the xvec vector with the assignment, as follows:

```
x1, x2, v1, v2 = xvec
```

This is not strictly necessary but improves readability. We then compute the auxiliary quantity, d (this is the denominator of the last two equations). Finally, the output array is computed according to the formulae in the system. Note that no derivatives are computed since all information that is needed by the solver is contained in the right-hand side of the equations.

We are now ready to solve the system of differential equations using the following lines of code:

```
import scipy.integrate as integrate
earth_radius = 6.371E6
v0 = 8500
h0 = 5E5
ic = array([0.0, earth_radius + h0, v0, 0.0])
tmax = 8700.0
dt = 10.0
tvalues = arange(0.0, tmax, dt)
xsol = integrate.odeint(ode_func, ic, tvalues)
```

The first line of the preceding code imports the integrate module, where the differential equations are solved. We then need to specify the initial position and velocity of the projectile. We assume that the canon is at the North Pole, atop a tower of 50,000 m (although this is clearly unrealistic, we just choose such a large value to enhance the visibility of the orbit). Since Earth is not a perfect sphere, we use an average value for the radius. The initial velocity is set to 8500 m/s.

The initial conditions are stored in a NumPy array with the following assignment:

```
ic = array([0.0, earth_radius + h0, v0, 0.0])
```

The next step is to define the initial time (zero in our case) and the array of times at which the solution is sought. This is done with the following three lines of code:

```
tmax = 8650.0
dt = 60.0
tvalues = arange(0.0, tmax, dt)
```

We first define tmax as being the duration of the simulation (in seconds). The variable dt stores the time intervals at which we want to record the solution. In the preceding code, the solution will be recorded every 60 seconds for 8,650 seconds. The final time was chosen by trial-and-error to correspond, approximately, to one orbit of the projectile.

We are now ready to compute the solution, which is done with a call to the odeint() function. The solution is stored in the vector, xsol, which has one row for each time at which the solution is computed. To see the first few rows of the vector, we can run the following command:

```
xsol[:10]
```

The preceding command produces the following output:

```
array([[  0.00000000e+00,   6.87100000e+06,   8.50000000e+03,
          0.00000000e+00],
       [  5.09624253e+05,   6.85581217e+06,   8.48122162e+03,
         -5.05935282e+02],
       [  1.01700042e+06,   6.81036510e+06,   8.42515172e+03,
         -1.00800330e+03],
       [  1.51991202e+06,   6.73500470e+06,   8.33257580e+03,
         -1.50243025e+03],
       [  2.01620463e+06,   6.63029830e+06,   8.20477026e+03,
         -1.98562415e+03],
       [  2.50381401e+06,   6.49702131e+06,   8.04345585e+03,
         -2.45425372e+03],
       [  2.98079103e+06,   6.33613950e+06,   7.85073707e+03,
         -2.90531389e+03],
       [  3.44532256e+06,   6.14878788e+06,   7.62903174e+03,
         -3.33617549e+03],
```

```
[  3.89574810e+06,   5.93624710e+06,   7.38099497e+03,
  -3.74461812e+03],
[  4.33057158e+06,   5.69991830e+06,   7.10944180e+03,
  -4.12884566e+03]])
```

These values are the position and velocity vectors of the projectile from time 0 s to time 360 s at intervals of 60 s.

We definitely want to produce a plot of the orbit. This can be done by running the following code in a cell:

```
subplot(111, aspect='equal')
axis(earth_radius * array([-1.5, 1.5, -1.8, 1.2]))
earth = Circle((0.,0.),
               earth_radius,
               ec='Black', fc='Brown', lw=3)
gca().add_artist(earth)
plot(xsol[:,0], xsol[:,1], lw=2, color='DarkBlue')
title('Newton\'s Canon, $v_0={}$ m/s'.format(v0))
```

We want to use the same scale in both axes since both axes represent spatial coordinates in meters. This is done in the first line of code. The second line sets the axis limits so that the plot of the orbit fits comfortably in the picture.

Then, we plot a circle to represent Earth using the following lines of code:

```
earth = Circle((0.,0.),
               earth_radius,
               ec='Black', fc='Brown', lw=3)
gca().add_artist(earth)
```

We have not emphasized using `Artist` objects in our plots since these are at a lower level than is usually required for scientific plots. Here, we are constructing a `Circle` object by giving its center, radius, and appearance options: a black edge color, brown face color, and a line width equal to 3. The second line of code shows how to add the `Circle` object to the plot.

After drawing Earth, we plot the orbit using the following line of code:

```
plot(xsol[:,0], xsol[:,1], lw=2, color='DarkBlue')
```

This is a standard call to the `plot()` function. Note that we plot only the first two columns of the `xsol` array since these represent the position of the projectile (recall that the other two represent the velocity). The following image is what we get as the output:

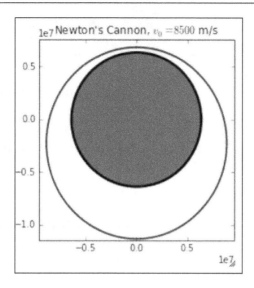

A numerical solution for differential equations is a sophisticated topic, and a complete treatment of the issue is beyond the scope of this book, but we will present the full form of the `odeint()` function and comment on some of the options. The `odeint()` function is a Python wrapper on the `lsoda` solver from ODEPACK, the Fortran library. Detailed information about the solver can be found at http://people.sc.fsu.edu/~jburkardt/f77_src/odepack/odepack.html

The following lines of code are the complete signature of `odeint()`:

```
odeint(ode_func, x0, tvalues, args=(), Dfun=None, col_deriv=0,
       full_output=0, ml=None, mu=None, rtol=None, atol=None,
       tcrit=None, h0=0.0, hmax=0.0, hmin=0.0,ixpr=0, mxstep=0,
       mxhnil=0, mxordn=12, mxords=5, printmessg=0)
```

The arguments, `ode_func`, `x0` and `tvalues`, have already been discussed. The argument `args` allows us to pass extra parameters to the equation being solved. This is a very common situation, which is illustrated in the next example. In this case, the function defining the system must have the following signature:

```
ode_func(x, t, p1, p2, ... , pn)
```

Here, `p1`, `p2`, and `pn` are extra parameters. These parameters are fixed for a single solution but can change from one solution to the other (they are normally used to represent the environment). The tuple passed to `args` must have a length exactly equal to the number of parameters that `ode_func()` requires.

The following is a partial list of the meaning of the most common options:

- `Dfun` is a function that computes the Jacobian of the system. This may improve the accuracy of the solution.
- Whether the Jacobian has the derivatives of the right-hand side along its columns (`True`, faster) or rows (`False`) is specified by `col_deriv`.
- If `full_output` is set to `True`, the output contains diagnostics about the solution process. This may be useful if errors accumulate and the solution process is not successfully completed.

In the last example in this section, we present the Lorenz oscillator, a simplified model for atmospheric convection, and a famous equation that displays chaotic behavior for certain values of the parameters. We will also use this example to demonstrate how to plot solutions in three dimensions.

The Lorenz system is defined by the following equations:

$$\frac{dx}{dt} = \sigma(y - x)$$

$$\frac{dy}{dt} = x(\rho - z) - y$$

$$\frac{dz}{dt} = xy - \beta z$$

We start by defining a Python function representing the system, as follows:

```
def ode_func(xvec, t, sigma, rho, beta):
    x, y, z = xvec
    return array([sigma * (y - x),
                  x * (rho - z) - y,
                  x * y - beta * z ])
```

The only difference between this system and the previous one is the presence of the parameters `sigma`, `rho`, and `beta`. Note that they are just added as extra arguments to `ode_func()`. Solving the equation is almost the same as solving the previous example:

```
tmax = 50
tdelta = 0.005
tvalues = arange(0, tmax, tdelta)
ic = array([0.0, 1.0, 0.0])
sol = integrate.odeint(ode_func, ic, tvalues,
                       args=(10., 28., 8./3.))
```

We define the array of times and the initial condition just as we did in the previous example. Notice that since this is a three-dimensional problem, there are initial conditions in an array with three components. Then comes the call to `odeint()`. The call now has an extra argument:

```
args=(10., 28., 8./3.)
```

This sets `sigma`, `rho`, and `beta`, respectively, to the values `10`, `28`, and `8/3`. These are values that are known to correspond to chaotic solutions.

The solution can then be plotted with the following code:

```
from mpl_toolkits.mplot3d import Axes3D
fig = plt.figure(figsize=(8,8))
from mpl_toolkits.mplot3d import Axes3D
fig = plt.figure(figsize=(8,8))
ax = fig.add_subplot(111, projection='3d')
x, y, z = sol.transpose()
ax.plot(x, y, z, lw=0.5, color='DarkBlue')
ax.set_xlabel('$x$')
ax.set_ylabel('$y$')
ax.set_zlabel('$z$')
```

The first three lines of code set up the axes for three-dimensional plotting. The next line extracts the data in a format suitable for plotting:

```
x, y, z = sol.transpose()
```

This code illustrates a common pattern. The array `sol` contains the coordinates of the solutions along its columns, so we transpose the array so that the data is along the rows of the array, and then assign each row to one of the variables x, y, and z.

The other lines of code are pretty straightforward: we call the `plot()` function and then add labels to the axes. The following is the figure that we get as the output:

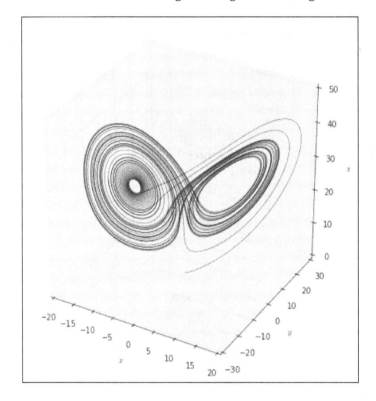

The preceding image is known as the classical Lorenz butterfly, a striking example of a strange attractor.

Accelerating computations with Numba and NumbaPro

In this section, we will discuss Numba and NumbaPro, two very exciting libraries to accelerate the NumPy code. Numba and NumbaPro were created by *Continuum Analytics*, the same company that produces the Anaconda distribution. Numba is part of the standard Anaconda distribution, but NumbaPro is a commercial product that must be purchased separately as part of the Accelerate package. However, NumbaPro can be downloaded for a free trial period.

These libraries are unique in that they allow the acceleration of code with the addition of a few lines of code. As the first example, let's consider the following lines of code to multiply two matrices:

```
def matrix_multiply(A, B):
    m, n = A.shape
    n, r = B.shape
    C = zeros((m, r), float64)
    for i in range(m):
        for j in range(r):
            acc = 0
            for k in range(n):
                acc += A[i, k] * B[k, j]
            C[i, j] = acc
    return C
```

The preceding code uses the straightforward definition of matrix multiplication and looks very much like code that would be written if we were implementing the algorithm in C. It is not Python-like and definitely not optimized. (In a real-world situation, one would simply use the NumPy built-in matrix multiplication.) Note, in particular, that the dimensions of the matrices are not checked: it is assumed that the number of columns of A is equal to the number of rows of B.

Let's first try the computation with small matrices, as follows:

```
A = array([[1,2,0],[1,-3,4],[0,-2,1],[3,7,-4]], dtype=float64)
B = array([[3,4],[-2,0],[2,4]], dtype = float64)
C = matrix_multiply(A, B)
print A
print B
print C
```

We start by defining the matrices A and B (note that the dimensions are compatible for multiplication). As in all examples in this section, we are careful to include a data type specification (this may improve optimization). Then, we simply call matrix_multiply, store the result in the array C, and print the three matrices. The result is the following:

```
[[ 1.    2.    0.]
 [ 1.   -3.    4.]
 [ 0.   -2.    1.]
 [ 3.    7.   -4.]]
[[ 3    4]
```

```
[ -2     0]
[  2     4]]
[[ -1.    4.]
 [  17.  20.]
 [  6.    4.]
 [ -13. -4.]]
```

You can verify that the algorithm is correct by manually checking a few entries. Alternatively, we can check whether the result agrees with the built-in matrix multiplication, as follows:

```
C - A.dot(B)
array([[ 0. ,   0.],
       [ 0. ,   0.],
       [ 0. ,   0.],
       [ 0. ,   0.]])
```

Everything seems to be fine. Now, we want to define some larger random matrices, as follows:

```
n = 100
A = rand(n, n)
B = rand(n, n)
```

In a 64-bit architecture, the preceding lines of code will automatically produce matrices of 64-bit floats. Next, we multiply the matrices and time the result as follows:

```
%%timeit
C = matrix_multiply(A, B)
```

The output of the preceding computation is as follows:

```
1 loops, best of 3: 472 ms per loop
```

The timing results will, of course, differ depending on the machine running the code. This example was run on an Intel Core i7 processor at 3.5 GHz with 16 GB of memory running a Microsoft Windows 7, 64-bit operating system.

Let's now see how we can quickly optimize this function. First, load the jit function from the Numba module, as follows:

```
from numba import jit
```

Then, define the function with the @jit decorator preceding it, as follows:

```
@jit
```

```
def matrix_multiply_jit(A, B):
    m, n = A.shape
    n, r = B.shape
    C = zeros((m, r), float64)
    for i in range(m):
        for j in range(r):
            acc = 0
            for k in range(n):
                acc += A[i, k] * B[k, j]
            C[i, j] = acc
    return C
```

Note that the only change to the code is the addition of the decorator. (We also changed the name of the function to avoid confusion, but this is not necessary.) Decorators are an advanced Python topic, but we do not need to go into the details of how they work. More information about decorators is available in the excellent blog postings by Simeon Franklin at `http://simeonfranklin.com/blog/2012/jul/1/python-decorators-in-12-steps/`.

Let's now time our code, as follows:

```
%%timeit
C = matrix_multiply_jit(A, B)
```

The following is the resultant output:

```
1000 loops, best of 3: 1.8 ms per loop
```

This is a 260-fold improvement with a single line of code! You should keep things in perspective here since this kind of acceleration cannot be expected for generic code. Remember that we wrote our code purposefully in a way that does not use the already-optimized functions from NumPy. For the sake of comparison and full disclosure, let's compare this with the built-in `dot()` method:

```
%%timeit
C = A.dot(B)
```

The resultant output is as follows:

```
10000 loops, best of 3: 28.6 µs per loop
```

So, even with acceleration, our function cannot compete with built-in NumPy. We emphasize again that the goal of this section is to present an overview of acceleration techniques and not delve deeply into sophisticated optimization methods.

It is worth having some understanding of how the @jit decorator works. When a function decorated by @jit is called, the library attempts to infer the data type of the arguments and return value, and on the fly produces a compiled version of the function and then calls it. The result is a function call that is comparable to code written in C.

Instead of letting the type of arguments and return value be inferred, it is possible to specify the data types, which may result in improved performance. The following table consists of the data types supported and the abbreviations used by Numba:

Data type	Abbreviation
boolean	b1
bool_	b1
byte	u1
uint8	u1
uint16	u2
uint32	u4
uint64	u8
char	i1
int8	i1
int16	i2
int32	i4
int64	i8
float_	f4
float32	f4
double	f8
float64	f8
complex64	c8
complex128	c16

These names are all defined in the Numba module. For example, to define a function that adds two floating-point values, we use the following code:

```
from numba import jit, f8
@jit (f8(f8,f8))
def my_sum(a, b):
    return a + b
```

Note the decorator syntax, which is as follows:

```
@jit (f8(f8,f8))
```

This specifies a function that takes two `float64` arguments and returns a `float64` value. The function is then called, as follows:

```
my_sum(3.5, 6.9)
```

This produces the expected result. However, if we try something like the following code, we get an error:

```
a = array([1.4, 2.0])
b = array([2.3, 5,2])
my_sum(a,b)
```

It is, however, possible to use arrays with the `@jit` decorator. To define a function that adds two one-dimensional arrays, one would use the following lines of code:

```
@jit (f8[:](f8[:],f8[:]))
def vector_sum(a, b):
    return a + b
```

Note how a vector is specified. A two-dimensional array is denoted by `f8[:,:]`, a three-dimensional array by `f8[:,:,:]`, and so on.

`NumbaPro` is the commercial version of `Numba` and adds several enhancements. We will focus on parallel processing using the **Graphics Processing Unit (GPU)** as an example of an exciting new technology that is made easily available in a notebook.

To run the examples that follow, the reader must have `NumbaPro`, a CUDA-compatible GPU (henceforth called the "device"), and the latest CUDA-compatible driver.

A list of CUDA-compatible devices can be found at `https://developer.nvidia.com/cuda-gpus`. After verifying that you have a compatible device, download and install the latest version of the CUDA SDK from `https://developer.nvidia.com/cuda-downloads` for the appropriate platform. The CUDA toolkit comes with several examples that you can use to test the installation.

The `NumbaPro` download is available at `https://store.continuum.io/cshop/accelerate/`. Download and install the `Accelerate` library.

To test the setup, start an IPython notebook and run the following in a cell:

```
import numbapro
numbapro.check_cuda()
```

If everything is fine, this will print a list of the CUDA libraries installed by Anaconda as well as a list of the CUDA-compatible devices available in your system. You will also see a PASSED message at the end of the display.

Even though CUDA programming is a relatively easy path to massive parallelism, there are still some concepts that have to be mastered before we can tackle our first CUDA program. We will outline the basics of the architecture here, discussing only enough to run the examples that follow. For a complete specification, see the **CUDA Programming Guide**, available at `http://docs.nvidia.com/cuda/cuda-c-programming-guide/index.html#programming-model`.

GPUs were originally designed to process rendering operations with greater speed than the computer's CPU is capable of. This processing acceleration is achieved, in large measure, by massively parallelizing the graphical operations required by the rendering pipeline.

A CUDA-compatible GPU consists of an array of **Streaming Multiprocessors (SMs)**. Each one of the SMs, by itself, cannot compete with current CPUs in terms of speed. However, the fact that many SMs can cooperate to solve a problem more than compensates for that. The SMs can also access memory that resides in the GPU, referred to as *device memory*.

In CUDA, there is a strict separation between code that runs in the CPU and code that runs in the device (the GPU). One particular restriction is that while CPU code can only access regular computer memory, device code can only access device memory. Code that runs in the device is specified in a function called a *kernel*. The kernel is compiled into a low-level language that is understood by the SMs and runs into each SM asynchronously (meaning that each SM proceeds at its own pace unless special synchronization instructions are found). Thus, a simple computation in CUDA usually requires the following three steps:

1. Transfer input data from the computer memory to the device memory.
2. Launch the kernel in the device.
3. Transfer output data from the device memory to the computer memory so that it is accessible to the CPU again.

As you will see, the memory transfers are made transparent by Python CUDA. (There is still the possibility to control it programmatically if needed.)

The kernel is launched simultaneously in an array of SMs, and each thread proceeds independently with the computation. Each SM can run several threads in parallel and can access all the device's memory. (The architecture is more complicated, and there are other kinds of memory available that will not be discussed here.) In the simplest case, each thread will access only a few memory areas, each containing a 64-bit floating value, and the memory accessed by a thread is never accessed by any other thread. So, there is no need for synchronization. In more complex problems, synchronization may be a major issue.

The set of threads being run features a two-level array structure:

- Threads are organized in **blocks**. Each block is an array of threads with up to 3 dimensions The dimensions of a block are stored in a variable called `blockDim`. Threads in a block are identified by the variable, `threadIdx`. This is a structure with three integer fields: `threadIdx.x`, `threadIdx.y`, and `threadIdx.z`. These fields uniquely identify each thread in the block.
- Blocks are organized in a **grid**. The grid is an array of blocks with up to 3 dimensions. The dimensions of the grid are stored in a variable called `gridDim`. Blocks in a grid are identified by the variable, `gridIdx`. This is a structure with three integer fields: `gridIdx.x`, `gridIdx.y`, and `gridIdx.z`. These fields uniquely identify each block in the grid.

An example of this organizational structure is given in the following figure:

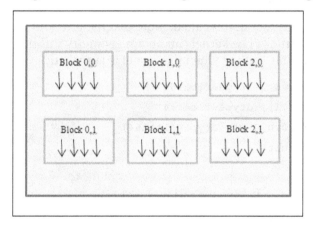

In the preceding example, `gridDim` is (2, 3, 1) since there are two rows and three columns of blocks (and a single space dimension). All the blocks in the grid are one-dimensional, so `blockDim` is (4, 1, 1). The third thread in the first block of the bottom row, for example, is identified by the following lines of code:

```
blockIdx.x=0, blockIdx.y=1, blockIdx.z=1
threadIdx.x=2, threadIdx.y=1, threadIdx.z=1
```

At runtime, each individual thread has access to this identifying information.

A key point of the CUDA architecture is the following:

- All threads in the same block always run concurrently in a single SM until all threads in the block have terminated
- Different blocks can run concurrently or serially depending on the availability of an SM to carry out the computation

We are now ready to define the kernel using Python CUDA. We will write a function that computes the sum of two vectors in the GPU. Run the following code in a cell:

```
from numbapro import cuda
@cuda.jit('void(float64[:], float64[:], float64[:])')
def sum(a, b, result):
    i = cuda.threadIdx.x
    result[i] = a[i] + b[i]
```

We assume that there is only one block of threads, and each thread is responsible for adding the elements of the array at a single position. The array position that a thread is responsible for is identified by the value of threadIdx.x. Note that the kernel has no return value. We need to specify an array, result, to hold the return value of the computation.

Let's now see how this function is called. Note that the grid and block geometry is not defined in the kernel. (The kernel can obtain geometry information if necessary; more on that later.) This is done when the kernel is launched:

```
a = array([1,2,3,4,5], dtype=float64)
b = array([5,4,3,2,1], dtype=float64)
result = array([0,0,0,0,0], dtype=float64)
sum[1,5](a, b, result)
print result
```

The preceding lines of code give the following output:

```
[ 6.  6.  6.  6.  6.]
```

The main point in this code is the following line:

```
sum[1,5](a, b, result)
```

The preceding line launches the kernel in a grid with 1 block, with 5 threads in the block. Both the grid and the blocks are one-dimensional. Let's now add larger vectors:

```
n = 64
a = arange(0,n,dtype=float64)
b = arange(n,0,-1, dtype=float64)
result = zeros(n,dtype=float64)
sum[1,n](a, b, result)
print result[:5]
```

The preceding lines of code are essentially the same as before but a little more generic in that the size of the array can be changed. What we want to do is increase the size of n. If you try a value such as n=10000, an error of type CUDA_ERROR_INVALID_VALUE occurs. The problem is that there is a hard limit on the number of threads that can be run by a single SM, that is, there is a limit to the number of threads that can be executed in a single block. To be able to handle large vectors, we need to modify the code so that it can handle multiple blocks. To this end, change the definition of the sum() function in the following way:

```
from numbapro import cuda
@cuda.jit('void(float64[:], float64[:], float64[:], int32)')
def sum(a, b, result, n):
    tx = cuda.threadIdx.x
    bx = cuda.blockIdx.x
    bsz = cuda.blockDim.x
    i = tx + bx * bsz
    if i < n:
        result[i] = a[i] + b[i]
```

The first thing to note is that we include an argument of type int32 to hold the size of the arrays being added. The main point now is that threads in different blocks must address different areas of memory, so the computation of the index i associated to a thread is more complicated. Essentially, we must know the number of blocks that come before the current block, multiply that by the block dimension, and add the current thread index. Then, before adding the relevant memory positions, we check if the index is valid. This prevents the thread from accessing areas that are not part of the input/output arrays and is an essential check in more complex code. To test the code, run the following:

```
n = 100000
a = arange(0,n,dtype=float64)
b = arange(n,0,-1, dtype=float64)
result = zeros(n,dtype=float64)
sum[1000,64](a, b, result, n)
print result[:5]
```

The preceding code should run without a hitch. Note that we are specifying a grid with 1000 blocks and 64 threads per block. The number of blocks in a grid is unlimited, the device being responsible for allocating the SMs in an optimal way. Note that the number of blocks must be large enough to cover the input/output arrays. In our case, this means blockDim.x * gridDim.x >= n.

We are now ready to compute with large vectors. Try the following code:

```
n = 100000
a = rand(n)
b = rand(n)
result = zeros(n, dtype=float64)
bd = 10000
gd = 64
if bd * gd < n:
    print 'Block/grid dimensions too small'
else:
    sum[bd,gd](a, b, result, n)
print result[:10]
```

The reader should experiment with different values of n, bd, and gd. Remember that the maximum value of gd depends on the device in your computer. An interesting experiment is to check how the computation scales for larger values of n.

Summary

In this chapter, we covered the use of advanced mathematical algorithms in SciPy, including solving equations and finding optimal values, integration, and differential equations. The chapter concluded with a discussion on using parallelization in the GPU to accelerate computations.

A
IPython Notebook Reference Card

Starting the notebook

To start the notebook, open a terminal window and run the following command:

```
ipython notebook
```

It is important that you are in the directory that contains your notebooks when you run the preceding command.

Keyboard shortcuts

Some of the important keyboard shortcuts are as follows:

- To go into the Edit mode, press *Enter* or click on the cell
- To go into the Command mode, press *Esc*

Shortcuts in the Edit mode

Some of the important shortcuts used in the Edit mode are as follows:

- To run a cell, the following shortcuts are used:
    - To run a cell and move to the next cell, press *Shift + Enter*
    - To run a cell, but stay in the same cell, press *Ctrl + Enter*
    - To run a cell and insert a new cell below it, press *Alt + Enter*
    - To create a new line in the current cell, press *Enter*

- To indent the content, press *Tab*
- To start code completion, start typing in the cell and then press *Tab*
- To select all, press *Ctrl + A*
- To undo an action, press *Ctrl + Z*
- To redo an action, press *Ctrl + Y* or *Ctrl + Shift + Z*
- To go to the start of the cell, press *Ctrl + Home*
- To go to the end of the cell, press *Ctrl + End*
- To split a cell, press *Ctrl + Shift + -*

Shortcuts in the Command mode

- To list the keyboard shortcuts, press *H*
- To change the cell mode to one of the following, the shortcuts are as follows:
  - **Code**: Press *Y*
  - **Markdown**: Press *M*
  - **Heading**: Press a number between *1* and *6*, according to the heading size
  - **Raw NBConvert**: Press *R*
- To select a cell above the current cell, press the Up key or *K*
- To select a cell below the current cell, press the Down key or *J*
- To move a cell up by one position, press *Ctrl + K*
- To move a cell down by one position, press *Ctrl + J*
- To insert a new cell above the current cell, press *A*
- To insert a new cell below the current cell, press *B*
- To cut a cell, press *X*
- To copy a cell, press *C*
- To paste a cell below the current cell, press *V*
- To paste a cell above the current cell, press *Shift + V*
- To delete a cell, press *D*
- To undo a delete action, press *Z*
- To merge the current cell with the cell below it, press *Shift + M*
- To toggle line numbers, press *L*

Importing modules

The steps to load some of the important modules are as follows:

- To load NumPy and matplotlib to work interactively, along with inline graphics, run the following command:

  ```
  pylab inline
  ```

- To load NumPy and matplotlib without importing names into the current namespace, with inline graphics, run the following command line:

  ```
  pylab --no-import-all inline
  ```

- To load SciPy modules, use any of the following standard Python import commands:

  ```
  import scipy.<module>
  import scipy.<module> as <local-name>
  from scipy.<module> import <function>
  ```

If the -no-import-all options is used, the functions and objects have to be prefixed by the appropriate module name as follows:

- For NumPy functions and objects, use numpy or np.
- For interactive graphics, use pyplot or plt.

Modules from libraries installed in the system as well as the user-created modules with the .py extension can be imported through the standard Python mechanism.

Getting help

There are a number of ways to get help:

- To start interactive help, run the following command:

  ```
  help()
  ```

- To get help with a function or object, run the following command:

  ```
  help(object)
  help(function)
  <object>?
  <function>?
  ```

- For tab completion, start typing the name of the function/object/method and press *Tab*.

- To get a tooltip, start typing the name of the function/object/method and press *Shift + Tab*.

B
A Brief Review of Python

Introduction

This appendix will give you a brief tour of the Python syntax. This is not intended to be a course on Python programming, but can be used by readers who are unfamiliar with the language as a quick introduction. The following topics will be covered in this appendix:

- Basic types, expressions, and variables and their assignment
- Sequence types
- Dictionaries
- Control structures
- Functions, objects, and methods

Basic types, expressions, and variables and their assignment

Any data that can be referred to in a Python code is considered an **object**. Objects are used to represent everything from *atomic* data, such as numbers, to very complex data structures, such as multidimensional arrays, database connections, and documents in several formats.

At the root of the object hierarchy are the numeric data types. These include the following:

- **Integers**: There are three types of integers in Python.

    ○ **Plain integers**: They are represented in the native architecture, which, in most systems, will be either 32- or 64-bit signed values.

    ○ **Long integers**: They are integers with unlimited range, subject to available memory. Most of the time, the programmer does not need to be concerned with the distinction between plain and long integers. Python deals with conversions between the types in a transparent way.

    ○ **Booleans**: They represent the values `False` and `True`. In most situations, they are equivalent to `0` and `1`, respectively.

- **Floats**: They represent the native double-precision floating-point numbers.

- **Complex**: They represent complex numbers, represented as a pair of double-precision floating-point numbers.

The following table has examples of **literals** (that is, **constants**) for each data type:

Data type	Literals
Integers	0, 2, 4, ..., 43882838388
	5L, 5l (long integer)
	0xFE4 (hexadecimal)
	03241 (octal)
Real numbers (float)	5.34, 1.2, 3., 0
	1.4e-32 (scientific notation)
Complex	1.0+3.4j, 1+2j, 1j, 0j, complex(4.3, 2.5)

The imaginary unit is represented by `j`, but only if it follows a number literal (otherwise, it represents the variable named `j`). So, to represent the imaginary unit we must use `1j` and the complex zero is `0j`. The real and imaginary part of a complex number are always stored as double-precision floating-point values.

 Note that the set of numeric types is greatly extended by `NumPy` to allow efficient numeric computations.

The assignment statement is used to store values in variables, as follows:

```
a = 3
b = 2.28
c = 12
d = 1+2j
```

Python supports *multiple simultaneous assignments* of values, so the previous four lines of code could be equivalently written in a single line as follows:

```
a, b, c, d = 3, 2.28, 12, 1+2j
```

In a multiple assignment, all expressions in the right-hand side are evaluated before the assignments are made. For example, a common idiom to exchange the values of two variables is as follows:

```
v, w = w, v
```

As an exercise, the reader can try to predict the result of the following statement, given the preceding variable assignments:

```
a, b, c = a + b, c + d, a * b * c * d
print a, b, c, d
```

The following example shows how to compute the two solutions of a quadratic equation:

```
a, b, c = 2., -1., -4.
x1, x2 = .5 * (-b - (b ** 2 - 4 * a * c) ** 0.5), .5 * (-b + (b ** 2 - 4
* a * c) ** 0.5)
print x1, x2
```

Note that we force the variables a, b, and c to be floating-point values by using a decimal point. This is good practice when performing numerical computations. The following table contains a partial list of Python operators:

Operators	Python operators
Arithmetic	+ (Addition)
	- (Subtraction, unary minus)
	* (Multiplication)
	/ (Division, *see the note below the table*)
	// (Integer division)
	% (Remainder)

Operators	Python operators
Comparison	== (Equal to)
	> (Greater than)
	< (Less than)
	>= (Greater than or equal to)
	<= (Less than or equal to)
	!= (Not equal to)
Boolean	and
	or
	not
Bitwise Boolean	& (AND)
	| (OR)
	^ (XOR)
	~ (NOT)
Bitwise shift	<< (Left shift)
	>> (Right shift)

Care should be taken with the division operator (/). If the operands are integers, the result of this operation is the integer quotient. For example, 34/12 results 2. To get the floating point result, we must either enter floating point operands, as in 34./12., or add the following statement:

```
from __future__ import division
```

The // operator always represents integer division.

Arithmetic operators follow the rules for the order of operations that may be altered with the use of parenthesis. Comparison operators have lower precedence than arithmetic operators, and the or, and, and not operators have even lower precedence. So, an expression like the following one produces the expected result:

```
2 + 3 < 5 ** 2 and 4 * 3 != 13
```

In other words, the preceding command line is parsed as follows:

```
(((2 + 3) < (5 ** 2)) and ((4 * 3) != 13))
```

The logical operators and and or short circuit, so, for example, the second comparison is never evaluated in the command:

```
2 < 3 or 4 > 5
```

The precedence rules for the bitwise and shift operators may not be as intuitive, so it is recommended to always use parenthesis to specify the order of operations, which also adds clarity to the code.

Python also supports augmented assignments. For example, the following command lines first assign the value 5 to a, and then increment the value of a by one:

```
a = 5
a += 1
```

 Python does not have increment/decrement operators, such as a++ and ++a, as in the C language.

All Python operators have a corresponding augmented assignment statement. The general semantic for any operator $ is the following statement:

```
v $= <expression>
```

The preceding statement is equivalent to the following:

```
v = v $ (<expression>)
```

 Note that $ is not a valid Python operator, it is just being used as a placeholder for a generic operator.

Sequence types

Python sequence types are used to represent ordered collections of objects. They are classified into **mutable** and **immutable** sequence types. Here, we will only discuss `lists` (mutable) and `tuples` and `strings` (both immutable). Other sequence types are mentioned at the end of this section.

Lists

The following example shows how to construct a list in Python and assign it to a variable:

```
numbers = [0, 1.2, 234259399992, 4+3j]
```

Individual entries in the list are accessed with index notation as follows:

```
numbers[2]
```

Notice that indexing always starts with 0. Negative indices are allowed and they represent positions starting at the end of the list. For example, `numbers[-1]` is the last entry, `numbers[-2]` is the next-to-last entry, and so forth.

Since lists are a mutable sequence type, we are allowed to modify the entries in-place:

```
numbers[0] = -3
numbers[2] += numbers[0]
print numbers
```

Another important way to refer to elements in a Python sequence type is slices, which allow the extraction of sublists from a list. Since this topic is very important for NumPy arrays, we defer the discussion to *Appendix C, NumPy Arrays*.

Python lists have a nice set of features, a few of which are illustrated in the following code examples:

- To find the length of a list, use the following command:

  ```
  len(numbers)
  ```

- To reverse a list in place, use the following command:

  ```
  numbers.reverse()
  print numbers
  ```

- To append a new element, use the following command:

  ```
  numbers.append(35)
  print numbers
  ```

- To sort the list in-place, use the following command:

  ```
  values = [1.2, 0.5, -3.4, 12.6, 3.5]
  values.sort()
  print values
  values.sort(reverse=True)
  print values
  ```

- To insert a value at a position, use the following command:

  ```
  values.insert(3, 6.8)
  print values
  ```

- To extend a list, use the following command:

```
values.extend([7,8,9])
print values
```

Python has a few handy ways to construct frequently used lists. The `range()` function returns a list of equally spaced integers. The simplest form returns a list of successive integers starting at `0`:

```
range(10)
```

The preceding command returns the following list:

```
[0, 1, 2, 3, 4, 5, 6, 7, 8, 9]
```

Note that the last element is one less than the argument given in the function call. The rule of thumb is that `range(n)` returns a list with n elements starting at zero so that the last element is `n-1`. To start at a nonzero value, use the two-argument version as follows:

```
range(3, 17)
```

A third argument specifies an *increment*. The following command line produces a list of all positive multiples of 6 that are less than 100:

```
range(6,100,6)
```

Negative increments can also be used:

```
range(20, 2, -3)
```

Lists support concatenation, which is represented by the + operator:

```
l1 = range(1, 10)
l2 = range(10, 0, -1)
l3 = l1 + l2
print l3
```

 Note that for the NumPy arrays, the + operator is redefined to represent vector/matrix addition.

The multiplication operator (*) can be used to construct a list by repeating the elements of a given list, as follows:

```
l4 = 3*[4,-1,5]
print l4
```

The most flexible way to construct a list in Python is to use a list comprehension. A full discussion is beyond the scope of this appendix, but the following examples illustrate some of the possibilities:

- To display the list of the squares of the integers from 0 to 10 (inclusive), use the following command line:

```
[n ** 2 for n in range(11)]
```

- To display the list of divisors of an integer, use the following command lines:

```
k = 60
[d for d in range(1, k+1) if k % d == 0]
```

- To display the list of prime numbers up to 100, use the following command line (very inefficient):

```
[k for k in range(2,101) if len([d for d in range(1, k+1) if k % d
== 0])==2]
```

- To display the list of tuples of points with integers coordinates and their distances to the origin, use the following command line:

```
[(i,j,(i*i+j*j)**0.5) for i in range(5) for j in range(6)]
```

Tuples

Tuples are similar to lists, but are immutable — once created, their elements cannot be changed. The following command lines will result in an error message:

```
t1 = (2,3,5,7)
t1[2] = -4
```

Tuples have a few specialized uses in Python. They can be used as indexes in dictionaries (because they are immutable). They also consist of the mechanism that Python uses to return more than one value from a function. For example, the built-in function `divmod()` returns both the integer quotient and remainder in a tuple:

```
divmod(213, 43)
```

Tuples support the same sequence interface as lists, except for methods that would modify the tuple. For example, there is no method named `sort()` that sorts a tuple in place.

Strings

A Python string represents an immutable sequence of characters. There are two string types: `str`, representing ASCII strings, and `unicode`, representing Unicode strings.

A string literal is a sequence of characters enclosed by either single quotes or double quotes, as follows:

```
s1 = 'I am a string'
s2 = "I am a string"
print s1
print s2
```

There is no semantic difference between single quotes and double quotes, except that a single-quoted string can contain double quotes and a double quoted string can contain single quotes. For example, the following command lines are correct:

```
s3 = "I'm a string"
print s3
```

Strings are used for two main purposes: as dictionary indexes and to print messages. When printing messages, strings have the `format()` method that allows easy display of information. We use this feature frequently to add annotations to graphics. Here is an example:

```
n = 3
message = 'The square root of {:d} is approximately {:8.5f}.'.format(n, n ** 0.5)
print message
```

In the preceding example, there are two format specifiers:

- `{:d}`: This specifies a decimal format for an integer value
- `{:8.5f}`: This specifies a field of width 8 and 5 decimals for a floating-point value

The format specifications are matched (in order) with the arguments, in this case n and n ** 0.5.

Strings have a rich interface. If you need to code something with strings, it is very likely that there is a built-in function that does the job with very little modification. A list of all available string methods, as well as formatting features, is available at https://docs.python.org/2/library/stdtypes.html#string-methods.

Dictionaries

Python dictionaries are a data structure that contains key-item pairs. The keys must be immutable types, usually strings or tuples. Here is an example that shows how to construct a dictionary:

```
grades = {'Pete':87, 'Annie':92, 'Jodi':78}
```

To access an item, we provide the key as an index as follows:

```
print grades['Annie']
```

Dictionaries are mutable, so we can change the item values using them. If Jodi does extra work to improve her grade, we can change it as follows:

```
grades['Jodi'] += 10
print grades['Jodi']
```

To add an entry to a dictionary, just assign a value to a new key:

```
grades['Ivan']=94
```

However, attempting to access a nonexistent key yields an error.

An important point to realize is that dictionaries are not ordered. The following code is a standard idiom to iterate over a dictionary:

```
for key, item in grades.iteritems():
    print "{:s}'s grade in the test is {:d}".format(key, item)
```

The main point here is that the output is not at all related to the order in which the entries were added to the dictionary.

For more details on the dictionary interface, you can refer to `https://docs.python.org/2/library/stdtypes.html#mapping-types-dict`.

Control structures

Control structures allow changes to the flow of the execution of code. There are two types of structures that are of interest to us: **branching** and **looping**.

Branching allows the execution of different code depending on the result of a test. The following example shows an improved version of code to solve quadratic equations. An `if-then-else` structure is used to handle the cases of real and imaginary solutions, as follows:

```
a, b, c = 2., -4., 5.
```

```
discr = b ** 2 - 4 * a * c
if discr >= 0:
    sqroot = discr ** 0.5
    x1 = 0.5 * (-b + sqroot)
    x2 = 0.5 * (-b - sqroot)
else:
    sqroot = (-discr) ** 0.5
    x1 = 0.5 * (-b + sqroot * 1j)
    x2 = 0.5 * (-b - sqroot * 1j)
print x1, x2
```

The preceding code starts by computing the discriminant of the quadratic. Then, an if-then-else statement is used to decide if the roots are real or imaginary, according to the sign of the discriminant. Note the indentation of the code. Indentation is used in Python to define the boundaries of blocks of statements. The general form of the if-then-else structure is as follows:

```
if <condition>:
    <statement block T>
else:
    <statement block F>
```

First, the condition <condition> is evaluated. If it is True, the statement <statement block T> is executed. Otherwise, <statement block F> is executed. The else: clause can be omitted.

The most common looping structure in Python is the for statement. Here is an example:

```
numbers = [2, 4, 3, 6, 2, 1, 5, 10]
for n in numbers:
    r = n % 2
    if r == 0:
        print 'The integer {:d} is even'.format(n)
    else:
        print 'The integer {:d} is odd'.format(n)
```

We start by defining a list of integers. The for statement makes the variable n assume each value in the list numbers in succession and execute the indented block for each value. Note that there is an if-then-else structure inside the for loop. Also, the print statements are doubly-indented.

A `for` loop is frequently used to perform simple searches. A common scenario is the need to step out of the loop when a certain condition is met. The following code finds the first perfect square in a range of integers:

```
for n in range(30, 90):
    if int(n ** 0.5) ** 2 == n:
        print n
        break
```

For each value of n in the given range, we take the square root of n, take the integer part, and then calculate its square. If the result is equal to n, then we go into the `if` block, print n, and then break out of the loop.

What if there are no perfect squares in the range? Change the preceding function, `range(30, 60)`, to `range(125, 140)`. When the command line is run, nothing is printed, since there are no perfect squares between 125 and 140. Now, change the command line to the following:

```
for n in range(125, 140):
    if int(n ** 0.5) ** 2 == n:
        print n
        break
else:
    print 'There are no perfect squares in the range'
```

The `else` clause is only executed if the execution does not break out of the loop, in which case the message is printed.

Another frequent situation is when some values in the iteration must be skipped. In the following example, we print the square roots of a sequence of random numbers between -1 and 1, but only if the numbers are positive:

```
import random
numbers = [-1 + 2 * rand() for _ in range(20)]
for n in numbers:
    if n < 0:
        continue
    print 'The square root of {:8.6} is {:8.6}'.format(n, n ** 0.5)
```

When Python meets the `continue` statement in a loop, it skips the rest of the execution block and continues with the next value of the control variable.

Another control structure that is frequently used is the `while` loop. This structure executes a block of commands as long as a condition is true. For example, suppose we want to compute the running sum of a list of randomly generated values, but only until the sum is above a certain value. This can be done with the following code:

```
import random
bound = 10.
acc = 0.
n = 0
while acc < bound:
    v = random.random()
    acc += v
    print 'v={:5.4}, acc={:6.4}'.format(v, acc)
```

Another common situation that occurs more often than one might expect requires a pattern known as the **forever loop**. This happens when the condition to be checked is not available at the beginning of the loop. The following code, for example, implements the famous 3n+1 game:

```
n = 7
while True:
    if n % 2 == 0:
        n /= 2
    else:
        n = 3 * n + 1
    print n
    if n == 1:
        break
```

The game starts with an arbitrary integer, 7 in this case. Then, in each iteration, we test whether n is even. If it is, we divide it by 2; otherwise, multiply it by 3 and add 1. Then, we check whether we reached 1. If yes, we break from the loop. Since we don't know if we have to break until the end of the loop, we use a forever loop as follows:

```
while True:
    <statements>
    if <condition>:
        break
    <possibly more statements>
```

Some programmers avoid this construct, since it may easily lead to infinite loops if one is careless. However, it turns out to be very handy in certain situations. By the way, it is an open problem if the loop in the `3n+1` problem stops for all initial values! Readers may have some fun trying the initial value `n=27`.

Functions, objects, and methods

We now come to the constructs that really make Python so flexible and powerful, its object-oriented features. We have already seen some examples of object-oriented code in the previous sections (the object-oriented paradigm is so integral to Python that is hardly possible to write any code without using it), but now we will have a more specific treatment of these features.

Functions

We have already seen many examples of functions being used. For example, the `len()` function is used to compute the length of a list:

```
lst = range(1000)
print len(lst)
```

The most basic syntax for calling a function is as follows:

```
function_name(arg1, arg2, …, argn)
```

In this case, `arg1, arg2, …, argn` are called **positional arguments**, since they are matched according to the position in which they appear. As an example, let's consider the built-in function, `pow()`. This function takes up to three arguments:

```
pow(b, n, m)
```

In this form, the preceding function uses an optimized algorithm to compute b raised to the power n modulo m. (If you are wondering, this is an important operation in public key cryptography, for example.) The arguments b, n, and m are associated by their position. For example, to compute 12 raised to the tenth power modulo 15, we use the following command:

```
pow(12, 10, 15)
```

Python also supports sequences of arguments of arbitrary size. For example, the `max()` function computes the maximum of an arbitrary sequence of values:

```
max(2,6,8,-3,3,4)
```

The preceding command returns the value 8.

A third way to pass arguments to a function is to use **keyword arguments**. This turns out to be very useful, since it is in general difficult to remember the exact order of positional arguments. (I would prefer not to write a function with more than three or four positional arguments, for example.)

For example, the built-in int () function can be used to convert a string to an integer. The optional keyword argument, base, lets us specify the base for conversion. For example, the following command line assigns to n, an integer given in base 2:

```
n = int('10111010100001', base=2)
print n
```

Keyword arguments always have a default value. In our example, if the base is not specified, it is assumed to be 10.

We often need to write our own functions. This is done with the keyword, def. As an example, let's consider writing code to implement the well-known bisection method to solve equations numerically. A possible solution is as follows:

```
def bisection(f, a, b, tol=1e-5, itermax=1000):
    fa = f(a)
    fb = f(b)
    if fa * fb > 0:
        raise ValueError('f(a) and f(b) must have opposite signs')
    niter = 0
    while abs(a-b) > tol and niter < itermax:
        m = 0.5 * (a + b)
        fm = f(m)
        if fm * fa < 0:
            b, fb = m, fm
        else:
            a, fa = m, fm
    return min(a, b), max(a, b)
```

The preceding function takes three important and necessary arguments:

- The f function accepts a float value as input and returns a float value as output
- The floating-point values, a and b, which specify an interval that contains a zero of the function

The other two arguments are optional. The argument `tol` specifies the desired tolerance in the result and `itermax` specifies the maximum number of iterations. To use the `bisection()` function, we must first define the function `f`. We will take the opportunity to display another way to define a function in Python, as follows:

```
from math import cos, pi
f = lambda x: cos(x) - x
```

We are now ready to call the function with the following command:

```
bisection(f, 0, pi/2)
```

The preceding function returns the following output:

```
(0.7390851262506977, 0.7390911183631504)
```

Note that we designed the function to return an interval containing the zero. The length of the interval is less than `tol`, unless the maximum number of iterations is reached. If we want a smaller tolerance, we could use the following function:

```
bisection(f, 0, pi/2, tol=1E-10)
```

Now, suppose that we are concerned with the time the computation is taking. We can limit the maximum number as follows:

```
bisection(f, 0, pi/2, itermax=10, tol=1E-20)
```

Note that the order in which the keyword arguments are given is irrelevant and the desired tolerance is not reached in the preceding example.

Objects and methods

Objects are the most general data abstraction in Python. Actually, in Python, everything is an object from the point of view of the programmer.

An object is nothing more than a collection of structured data, together with an interface to operate on this data. Objects are defined using the `class` construct, but our goal here is not to show how to define classes. Although designing a new class is an advanced topic, using existing classes is pretty straightforward.

As an example, let's explore the built-in type `str`. Let's start by defining a `str` object we can play with as follows:

```
message = 'Mathematics is the queen of science'
```

To start, let's convert the message to uppercase as follows:

```
message.upper()
```

We say that the preceding statement calls the `upper()` method of the `message` object. A method is simply a function that is associated to an object. The following are a few other methods of the `str` objects:

- To find the first occurrence of a substring (returns `-1` if the string is not found), use the following command line:

  ```
  message.find('queen')
  ```

- To split the string in words, use the following command line:

  ```
  words = message.split()
  print words
  ```

- To count the number of occurrences of s substring, use the following command line

  ```
  message.count('e')
  ```

- To replace a substring by something else, use the following command line:

  ```
  message.replace('Mathematics', 'Mme. Curie')
  ```

 Note that the preceding methods do not change the original string object, but return new modified strings. Strings are immutable. For mutable objects, methods are free to change the data in the object.

Summary

In this appendix, we gave an overview of the Python syntax and features, covering basic types, expressions, variables, and assignment, basic data structures, functions, objects, and methods.

C
NumPy Arrays

Introduction

Arrays are the fundamental data structure introduced by NumPy, and they are the base of all libraries for scientific computing and data analysis we discussed in this book. This appendix will give a brief overview of the following array features:

- Array creation and member access
- Indexing and slicing

Array creation and member access

NumPy arrays are objects of the ndarray class, which represents a fixed-size multidimensional collection of homogeneous data.

Here, we will assume that the NumPy library has been imported using the following command line:

```
import numpy as np
```

Once we have done that, we can create ndarray (from now on, informally called **array object** or simply **array**) from a list of lists as indicated in the following command line:

```
a = np.array([[-2,3,-4,0],[2,-7,0,0],[3,-4,2,1]],dtype=np.float64)
print a
```

Contrary to Python lists and tuples, all entries of an array object must be of the same type. The types themselves are represented by NumPy objects and are referred to as dtype (from data type) of the array. In the preceding example, we explicitly specify dtype as float64, which represents a 64-bit floating-point value.

Arrays have several attributes that give information about the data layout. The more commonly used ones are as follows:

- The shape of the array is computed using the following command:

```
a.shape
```

The preceding command returns the tuple (3, 4), since this is a two-dimensional array with three rows and four columns. Somewhat surprisingly, the shape attribute is not read-only and we can use it to *reshape* the array:

```
a.shape = (6,2)
print a
```

After running the preceding example, run a.shape(3,4) to return to the original dimensions.

- The number of dimensions of the array is obtained using the following command:

```
a.ndim
```

This, of course, returns 2. An important notion in NumPy is the idea of *axes* of an array. A two dimensional array has two axes, numbered 0 and 1. If we think of the array as representing a mathematical matrix, axis 0 is vertical and points down, and axis 1 is horizontal and points to the right. Certain array methods have an optional axis keyword argument that lets the user specify along which axis the operation is performed.

- To get the number of elements in the array, we can use the following command:

```
a.size
```

In the preceding example, the output returned is 12, as expected.

- One final attribute of arrays is computing the *transpose* of an array. This can be done using the following command:

```
b = a.T
print b
```

An important thing that this creates is a *view* of the array a. The NumPy package is designed to work efficiently with very large arrays, and in most cases, avoids making copies of data unless absolutely necessary, or is explicitly directed to do so.

- Run the following lines of code:

```
print a
b[1,2] = 11
print a
```

Note that the entry 2, 1 of the array a is changed, demonstrating that both variables, a and b, point to the same area in memory.

- An array with uninitialized data can be created with the empty() function as follows:

```
c = np.empty(shape=(3,2), dtype=np.float64)
print c
```

- Using uninitialized data is not recommended, so it is perhaps preferable to use either the zeros() or ones() function as follows:

  ○ To use the zeros() function, execute the following command lines:

  ```
  d = np.zeros(shape=(3,2), dtype=np.float64)
  print d
  ```

  ○ To use the ones() function, execute the following command lines:

  ```
  e = np.ones(shape=(3,2), dtype=np.float64)
  print e
  ```

There are also functions that create new arrays with the same shape and data type of an existing array:

```
a_like = np.zeros_like(a)
print a_like
```

- The functions ones_like() and empty_like() produce arrays of ones and uninitialized data with the same shape as a given array.
- NumPy also has the eye() function that returns an identity array of the given dimension and dtype:

```
f = np.eye(5, dtype=np.float64)
print f
```

The number of rows and columns do not have to be the same. In this case, the resulting matrix will only be a left- or right- identity, as applicable:

```
g = np.eye(5, 3, dtype=np.float64)
print g
```

- Arrays can also be created from existing data. The `copy()` function clones an array as follows:

```
aa = np.copy(a)
print a
print aa
```

- The `frombuffer()` function creates an array from an object that exposes the (one-dimensional) buffer interface. Here is an example:

```
ar = np.arange(0.0, 1.0, 0.1, dtype=np.float64)
v = np.frombuffer(ar)
v.shape = (2, 5)
print v
```

  The `arange()` function is a NumPy extension of the Python range. It has a similar syntax, but allows ranges of floating-point values.

- The `loadtxt()` function reads an array from a text file. Suppose the text file `matrix.txt` contains the following data:

```
 1.3   4.6   7.8
-3.6   0.4   3.54
 2.4   1.7   4.5
```

  Then, we can read the data with the following command:

```
h = np.loadtxt('matrix.txt', dtype=np.float64)
print h
```

- Arrays can also be saved and loaded in the `.npy` format:

```
np.save('matrix.npy',h)
hh = np.load('matrix.npy')
print hh
```

Indexing and Slicing

To illustrate indexing, let's first create an array with random data using the following command:

```
import numpy.random
a = np.random.rand(6,5)
print a
```

This creates an array of dimension (6,5) that contains random data. Individual elements of the array are accessed with the usual index notation, for example, a[2,4].

An important technique to manipulate data in NumPy is the use of **slices**. A slice can be thought of as a subarray of an array. For example, let's say we want to extract a subarray with the middle two rows and first two columns of the array a. Consider the following command lines:

```
b = a[2:4,0:2]
print b
```

Now, let's make a very important observation. *A slice is simply a view of an array, and no data is actually copied.* This can be seen by running the following commands:

```
b[0,0]=0
print a
```

So, changes in b affect the array a! If we really need a copy, we need to explicitly say we want one. This can be done using the following command line:

```
c = np.copy(a[2:4,0:2])
c[0,0] = -1
print a
```

In the slice notation i:j, we can omit either i or j, in which case the slice refers to the beginning or end of the corresponding axis:

```
print a[:4,3:]
```

Omitting both i and j refers to a whole axis:

```
print a[:,2:4]
```

Finally, we can use the notation i:j:k to specify a stride k in the slice. In the following example, we first create a larger random array to illustrate this:

```
a = np.random.rand(10,6)
print a
print
print a[1:7:2,5:0:-3]
```

Let's now consider slices of higher dimensional arrays. We will start by creating a really large three-dimensional array as follows:

```
d1, d2, d3 = 4, 5, 3
a = np.random.rand(d1, d2, d3)
print a
```

Suppose we want to extract all elements with index 1 in the last axis. This can be done easily using an ellipsis object as follows:

```
print a[...,1]
```

The preceding command line is equivalent to the following one:

```
print a[:,:,1]
```

It is also possible to augment the matrix along an axis when slicing, as follows:

```
print a[0, :, np.newaxis, 0]
```

Compare the output of the preceding command line with the output of the following:

```
print a[0, :, 0]
```

Index

Symbols

%alias magic 40
%echo magic 40
.iloc method 90
.ix method 90
%load magic 43
.loc method 89
%pylab magic command 12
%run magic 43
%timeit magic 34

A

Anaconda
  about 8
  installing 8
  URL 8
animations 71-77
annotate() function 64
annotate() function, options
  arrowprops 65
  fontsize 65
  horizontalalignment 65
  verticalalignment 65
annotations
  and text 62-66
append() method 82
arange() function 15, 20, 164
arithmetic operator 145
array creation 161-164
array object 161
automagic 40
ax.axhline() function 73
axis keyword 162

B

basic types 143-147
bisection() function 158
Bitwise Boolean 146
Bitwise shift operator 146
blocks 135
bob 73
boolean operator 146
booleans 144
branching 152
brentq() function 113
broadcasting 68
Brownian Motion (BM) 100

C

calculus computation 117-128
cell magic, supported languages
  %%bash 43
  %%cmd 43
  %%html 43
  %%HTML 43
  %%javascript 43
  %%latex 43
  %%perl 43
  %%powershell 43
  %%python2 43
  %%python3   43
  %%ruby 43
  %%svg 43
  %%SVG 43
Cell-oriented magic 33
cells, shortcuts
  A 28
  B 28

C 28
Ctrl + J 28
Ctrl + K 28
Ctrl + S 28
D (press twice) 28
Enter 28
Esc 28
H 28
S 28
Shift + V 28
V 28
X 28
cell types
  about 29-31
  code 32
  Heading 1 to Heading 6 32
  markdown 32
  Raw NBConvert 32
chained indexing
  URL 94
chained reference 90
checkpoint 38
clabel() method 70
class 21
class construct 158
clear_output() function 76
code cell 12
coffee cooling problem, example 12-22
colormap feature 69
Command mode
  about 24, 28, 29
  keyboard shortcuts, using 140
Comma-separated values (CSV) 102
comparison operator 146
complex 144
computational tools
  about 95-101
  built-in 95, 96
computations
  accelerating, with Numba 128-138
  accelerating, with NumbaPro 128-138
computations, notebook
  interrupting 25
contours() method 70
control structures
  about 152-155
  functions 156

methods 158, 159
objects 156, 158
cooling law 14
cooling_law() function 14, 17
CUDA-compatible devices
  URL 133
CUDA Programming Guide
  URL 134

D

data
  loading 41-46
  saving 41-46
DataFrame
  slicing 94, 95
DataFrame class 88-94
dataset 102
decorators
  Simeon Franklin, URL 131
Dfun 126
dictionaries, Python 152
dictionary interface
  URL 152
divmod() function 150
drift 100

E

Edit mode
  about 24-27
  keyboard shortcuts, using 139
else clause 154
empty_like() function 163
equations, SciPy
  solving 111-117
exercises, IPython notebook 22
expressions 143-147
eye() function 163

F

f function 157
first-class objects 54
floats 144
forever loop 155
for loop 154
format() method 151

format specifiers
  {:8.5f} 151
  {:d} 151
formatting features
  URL 151
for statement 153
frombuffer() function 164
fsurface() function 67
function factory
  about 54
  using 54
functions 156-158

G

gen() 118
Geometrical Brownian Motion (GBM)
  URL 99
Graphics Processing Unit (GPU) 133
graphics tools 95
grids
  about 135
  URL 62
Gross Domestic Product (GDP) 104-106

H

help, modules
  obtaining 141
Help menu
  using 25
HTML
  about 49-51
  color names, URL 57

I

images
  loading 47-49
immutable 147
indexing 164, 165
inline directive 12
instance 21
integers 144
interactive mode 53
int() function 157
ipython command 11

IPython magics
  about 33-37
  Cell-oriented 33
  Line-oriented 33
IPython notebook 7
ipython qtconsole command 11
itermax 158

J

JSON
  URL 38
julia command 45
Julia scripting language
  about 45
  URL 45

K

keyboard shortcuts
  about 139
  used, in Command mode 140
  used, in Edit mode 139
keyword arguments 157

L

labels
  adding 59-61
LaTeX
  about 31
  URL 31
legend
  adding 59-62
legend() function 62
len() function 156
Line-oriented magic 33
linspace() function 55
lists 147-149
literals
  examples 144
load() function 46
loadtxt() function 164
logistic growth
  formula 54
long integers 144
looping 152

M

magic commands 12
magics
  %alias 40
  %cd 40
  %echo 40
  %ls 40
  %mkdir 40
  %pwd 40
  %rmdir 40
  about 40
make_gen() function 118
make_logistic() function 54
Markdown language
  about 29
  features 31
markercolor option 59
marker option 59
markers
  URL 59
markersize option 59
markevery option 59
mathematical algorithms, SciPy 111
matplotlib
  grids, URL 62
matplotlib documentation
  URL 22
matplotlib functions 49
member access 161-164
meshgrid() function 20, 68
metadata 103
methods 21, 158, 159
modes, operation
  Command mode 24
  Edit mode 24
modules
  importing 141
mutable 147

N

namespace pollution 12
nbconvert utility 32, 38
Nelder-Mead method 116
Not a number (NaN) 83

notebook
  about 139
  cell types 29-31
  Command mode 28, 29
  computations, interrupting 25
  converting, to other formats 38
  creating 11, 12
  editing 23, 24
  Edit mode 25-27
  Help menu, using 25
  navigating 23, 24
  running 8, 9
  saving 37, 38
  Wakari account, creating 10, 11
Notebook Interface Tour
  URL 25
notebooks, publishing
  URL 38
Numba
  about 37
  computations, accelerating with 128-138
NumbaPro
  about 37
  computations, accelerating with 128-138
  URL 133
NumPy arrays 161

O

object hierarchy
  booleans 144
  complex 144
  floats 144
  integers 144
  long integers 144
  plain integers 144
objects 156, 158, 159
odeint() function 125, 127
ones() function 163
ones_like() function 163
operating system
  interacting with 37
  notebook, converting to other
    formats 38, 39
  notebook, saving 37, 38
  shell commands, running 39-41

optimal values, SciPy
  finding 111-117

P

pandas
  about 45, 79
  URL 102
peg 73
percentage drift parameter 99
percentage volatility parameter 99
plain integers 144
plot function 54-59
plot() function 16, 54, 56
plots
  URL 66
plot_surface() method 69
positional arguments 156
project page
  URL 29
p-values 97
Python operators
  arithmetic 145
  Bitwise Boolean 146
  Bitwise shift 146
  boolean 146
  comparison 146
Python scripts
  running 41-43

R

range() function 149
read_csv() method 103
reveal.js file
  URL 39
Rich Display system
  about 47
  HTML 49-51
  images, loading 47-49
  YouTube videos, loading 47-49
rod 73

S

SciPy
  about 109, 110

equations, solving 111-117
mathematical algorithms 111
optimal values, finding 111-117
scripts
  running 41
  running, in other languages 43-45
sequence types
  about 147
  lists 147-149
  strings 151
  tuples 150
Series class 79-87
shell commands
  running 39-41
sin() function 35
slicing
  about 79, 164, 165
  DataFrame 94, 95
Streaming Multiprocessors (SMs) 134
strings 151
subplot() function 67
SVG 44

T

tab completion 27
taxicab distance 114
t-distribution 97
temperature_difference() function 20
temp_mixture() function 17
test
  running 35
text
  and annotations 62-66
text() function 65
three-dimensional plots 66-70
title
  adding 59-61
tuples 150

U

unicode 151

V

variables 143-147

W

Wakari 8
Wakari account
  creating 10, 11
  URL 10

Y

YouTube videos
  loading 47-49

Z

zeros() function 163
Z-scores 97

Thank you for buying
IPython Notebook Essentials

About Packt Publishing

Packt, pronounced 'packed', published its first book "*Mastering phpMyAdmin for Effective MySQL Management*" in April 2004 and subsequently continued to specialize in publishing highly focused books on specific technologies and solutions.

Our books and publications share the experiences of your fellow IT professionals in adapting and customizing today's systems, applications, and frameworks. Our solution based books give you the knowledge and power to customize the software and technologies you're using to get the job done. Packt books are more specific and less general than the IT books you have seen in the past. Our unique business model allows us to bring you more focused information, giving you more of what you need to know, and less of what you don't.

Packt is a modern, yet unique publishing company, which focuses on producing quality, cutting-edge books for communities of developers, administrators, and newbies alike. For more information, please visit our website: www.packtpub.com.

About Packt Open Source

In 2010, Packt launched two new brands, Packt Open Source and Packt Enterprise, in order to continue its focus on specialization. This book is part of the Packt Open Source brand, home to books published on software built around Open Source licenses, and offering information to anybody from advanced developers to budding web designers. The Open Source brand also runs Packt's Open Source Royalty Scheme, by which Packt gives a royalty to each Open Source project about whose software a book is sold.

Writing for Packt

We welcome all inquiries from people who are interested in authoring. Book proposals should be sent to author@packtpub.com. If your book idea is still at an early stage and you would like to discuss it first before writing a formal book proposal, contact us; one of our commissioning editors will get in touch with you.

We're not just looking for published authors; if you have strong technical skills but no writing experience, our experienced editors can help you develop a writing career, or simply get some additional reward for your expertise.

Learning IPython for Interactive Computing and Data Visualization

ISBN: 978-1-78216-993-2   Paperback: 138 pages

Learn IPython for interactive Python programming, high-performance numerical computing, and data visualization

1. A practical step-by-step tutorial which will help you to replace the Python console with the powerful IPython command-line interface.

2. Use the IPython notebook to modernize the way you interact with Python.

3. Perform highly efficient computations with NumPy and pandas.

IPython Interactive Computing and Visualization Cookbook

ISBN: 978-1-78328-481-8   Paperback: 512 pages

Over 100 hands-on recipes to sharpen your skills in high-performance numerical computing and data science with Python

1. Leverage the new features of the IPython notebook for interactive web-based big data analysis and visualization.

2. Become an expert in high-performance computing and visualization for data analysis and scientific modeling.

3. A comprehensive coverage of scientific computing through many hands-on, example-driven recipes with detailed, step-by-step explanations.

Please check **www.PacktPub.com** for information on our titles

Instant SymPy Starter

ISBN: 978-1-78216-362-6   Paperback: 52 pages

Learn to use SymPy's symbolic engine to simplify Python calculations

1. Learn something new in an Instant!
   A short, fast, focused guide delivering immediate results.

2. Set up the best computing environment with IPython Notebook, SymPy, and all your favorite Python libraries.

3. Learn how to streamline your computations with computer algebra.

NumPy Cookbook

ISBN: 978-1-84951-892-5   Paperback: 226 pages

Over 70 interesting recipes for learning the Python open source mathematical library, NumPy

1. Do high performance calculations with clean and efficient NumPy code.

2. Analyze large sets of data with statistical functions.

3. Execute complex linear algebra and mathematical computations.

Please check **www.PacktPub.com** for information on our titles

www.ingramcontent.com/pod-product-compliance
Lightning Source LLC
Chambersburg PA
CBHW060131060326
40690CB00018B/3839